T0169361

Finding the Words

How to talk with children and teens about death,
suicide, funerals, homicide, cremation, and
other end-of-life matters

BY ALAN D. WOLFELT, PH.D., C.T.

Companion Press is dedicated to the education and support of both the bereaved and breavement caregivers. We believe that those who companion the bereaved by walking with them as they journey in grief have a wondrous opportunity: to help others embrace and grow through grief—and to lead fuller, more deeply lived lives themselves because of this important ministry.

For a complete catalog and ordering information, write or call or visit our website.

Companion
P R E S S

Companion Press
The Center for Loss and Life Transition

3735 Broken Bow Road | Fort Collins, CO 80526

Phone: (970) 226-6050 | Fax: 1-800-922-6051

drwolfelt@centerforloss.com | www.centerforloss.com

Companion Press is an imprint of the Center for Loss and Life Transition
3735 Broken Bow Road, Fort Collins, CO 80526
(970) 226-6050
www.centerforloss.com

Companion Press books may be purchased in bulk for sales promotions, premiums, or fundraisers. Please contact the publisher at the above address for more information.

Printed in the United States of America

18 17 16 15 14 13   5 4 3 2 1

ISBN 978-1-61722-189-7

Contents

"There can be no keener revelation of a society's soul than the way in which it treats its children."

— NELSON MANDELA

Introduction

I have had the privilege of companioning thousands of people on their grief journeys over the years, including many children and teens. It is an honor to be a part of the intimate workings of grief and mourning. With each new person I meet, I learn something about this necessary and important response to the death of someone loved. I believe I have an obligation to teach others what I have learned about the sacred journey we call grief.

We live in a society where people are encouraged to move *around* grief instead of *through* grief. I daresay that we as a North American culture have become confused. There's no time to grieve or mourn; rather, children and adults hear such messages as "Carry on," "Keep your chin up," "She's in a better place," and "You just need to let go." Our friends, family, coworkers, and acquaintances encourage us to stay busy and avoid the feelings grief brings. In fact, we get the message that *not* showing our feelings is being strong and a sign that we are "doing well."

I believe it would be accurate to say that we live in an "emotion-phobic" society. If you, or a child you care for, have experienced the recent death of someone you love, I strongly encourage you to stand against these social and cultural messages and instead embrace your normal and natural grief openly as you actively express your pain through mourning.

You and the grieving child must walk hand-in-hand through the wilderness of grief despite the scary, dark shapes that may line your path. It takes bravery to walk through grief and actively mourn. But if you can, the reward is reconciliation of the pain and the promise of a transcendent future filled with purpose and meaning.

Mourning is essential to healing

Authentic mourning—grief honestly expressed on the outside—demands that you slow down, befriend dark emotions, and seek and accept support. Over time, if you actively grieve and mourn, you will begin to acknowledge the death and appropriately shift the relationship to one of loving memory. You can never fully leave grief behind, but with time and care it can change from overwhelming and debilitating to survivable and sometimes even inspiring. This is as true for children as it is for adults.

Avoiding or suppressing grief is harmful—even to kids

While families may be tempted to make swift, clean breaks from their loss, it does not ultimately serve them. When people do not feel or act on their feelings, they become unable to be changed by them. Feelings do not just resolve on their own. If ignored, they get lodged deep in our hearts, spirits, and bodies and can cause harm in the form of physical ailments or an overall sense of sadness, hopelessness, numbness, or disconnection. In other words, unexpressed grief results in "chronic grief," sometimes resulting in depression, anxiety, disconnection from others, substance abuse, and fatigue. This "carried grief" results in a muting of one's spirit or "divine spark."

The saying "Time heals all wounds" is misleading, as the passing of time *without the willingness to experience grief and mourning* does not open us to healing.

THE DIFFERENCE BETWEEN GRIEF AND MOURNING
Grief is the internal thoughts and feelings of loss and
pain when someone loved dies. Mourning is the outward,
shared expression of that grief, or "grief gone public." All
children grieve when someone they love dies. But if they
are to heal and grow into their potential, they must be
provided a safe, accepting atmosphere in which to mourn.

Grief is a process, not an event

Grief does not end when the funeral is over or the belongings
dispersed. There are no timelines or set stages of grief. Mourners
don't follow any rules, and no two people will grieve in the same
way. Children, especially, are unique in their grief because their
age, stage of development, and life experiences thus far strongly
influence their ability to understand and integrate the grief that
has touched their young lives. That's why it is essential for
them to have loving, caring adults who are unafraid of
the pain and emotions a deep loss can bring. Adults who
can open to pain and have the patience to allow it to unfold
naturally are valuable and true "companions" to children in
grief. Since you have chosen this book, I commend you for your
bravery and willingness to walk alongside a child on his or her
journey through grief.

To "companion" grieving children means
to be an active participant in their healing.
When you companion a grieving child, you
allow yourself to learn from his unique
experiences. You let him be the teacher
instead of the other way around. You walk
beside him, not in front of or behind him.
You see the world from his eyes. You accept
his pain and the unique way he expresses
it as the way it should be without telling
him how he ought to feel or act. You
especially do not suggest "getting over" his
pain or denying his pain, as denying stops
the loss from integrating from his head to
his heart, leaving him stunted and unable
to embrace the fullness of life.

THE TENETS OF COMPANIONING THE BEREAVED

TENET ONE
Companioning is about being present to another person's pain; it is not about taking away the pain.

TENET TWO
Companioning is about going to the wilderness of the soul with another human being; it is not about thinking you are responsible for finding the way out.

TENET THREE
Companioning is about honoring the spirit; it is not about focusing on the intellect.

TENET FOUR
Companioning is about listening with the heart; it is not about analyzing with the head.

TENET FIVE
Companioning is about bearing witness to the struggles of others; it is not about judging or directing these struggles.

TENET SIX
Companioning is about walking alongside; it is not about leading.

TENET SEVEN
Companioning is about discovering the gifts of sacred silence; it is not about filling up every moment with words.

TENET EIGHT
Companioning is about being still; it is not about frantic movement forward.

TENET NINE
Companioning is about respecting disorder and confusion; it is not about imposing order and logic.

TENET TEN
Companioning is about learning from others; it is not about teaching them.

TENET ELEVEN
Companioning is about compassionate curiosity; it is not about expertise.

A note to you

This book is written as a quick reference guide on how to talk with children about death and other end-of-life matters. It is primarily designed for parents and other guardians, but it will also be useful to relatives, friends, teachers, coaches, mentors, counselors, and any adult who cares for or works with children. It offers dialogue you can use when talking with children of different ages about a variety of death situations. You can use these words directly or modify them to fit your speaking style. Please note that while some of the questions/answers are specific to certain death circumstances, many are interchangeable. Don't hesitate to flip through the book in search of other "words" that might pertain to your unique circumstances.

It is my hope that this book helps you start the conversations that will help your child navigate the confusing, difficult feelings of grief and turn that grief into active mourning. I thank you for having the fortitude and desire to companion the child you love through grief. That is an enormous gift, and the reward will be watching him grow and flourish despite his loss and the pain it brings.

"Children are the hands by which we take hold of heaven."

— HENRY WARD BEECHER

CHAPTER ONE

Children's grief— why it's unique

Death changes children. Because they are still taking form, children are much more malleable than adults. Loss acts as a carving tool that helps shape them. Children look to others to help define them as they grow. With death they not only lose someone they love but what feels like a part of who they are.

After a death, a child's internal world shifts and is never the same. She must learn to adjust to living without everything that person brought to her life. The person who died most likely had a unique relationship with her. They shared intimacies that only the two knew about. She depended on the person for certain things, and she may be unsure of who will fulfill those needs now.

Adults provide stability for the child and make the world feel safe. Maybe a grandmother always believed in her granddaughter, even when others doubted her. With the death, she may have not only lost her grandmother but also an important source of self-assurance that kept her feeling steady. Her loss is doubled, intensifying her grief and mourning—and the closer the relationship, the more profound the grief.

Of course, more children and teens than we can imagine experience ambivalent, conflicted, or abusive relationships. In these cases, when a death occurs the young person typically mourns the lack of what she wishes she could or should have had in the relationship. Such conflicted relationships also create very profound grief and can result in a natural complication of the mourning process.

It's tempting to try to shelter children from grief and mourning. After all, as adults it's our job to keep them safe and protected. Yet we must remember, despite what messages we hear from others or within our culture, hurting is a necessary part of the journey on the way to healing. People never "get over" the death of a loved one. To some extent, they carry that feeling of loss with them forever. That's not to say that children cannot heal from the death of someone they love. By experiencing their grief and actively mourning, they can go on to live full, meaningful lives. Therefore, as parents and caregivers, we must help them mourn well so they can go on to live and love well.

EXCLUSIVE FEATURES OF CHILDHOOD GRIEF

No two people experience grief in the same way, and for children this is doubly so. Their age, maturity, and emotional, mental, and spiritual development dictate the shape and form of their grief. A preschooler might protest his loss by wetting the bed again, while a teenager might try to drown his pain by drinking or taking on other risky behaviors. It has been my longstanding belief that any child old enough to love is old enough to grieve. All kids grieve (except those who experience the tragedy of attachment disorder), regardless of age. They just do so differently.

Personal development plays a large role in determining how the child might express, or move through, his grief. The relationship with the person who died, the nature of the death, and the child's gender and personality also play major roles in how he will grieve and mourn. Of course, these are not the only influences on how a child will view or experience death. Past experiences with death, how those around him deal with the death, and his own perceptions about death also influence his grief process — and make it uniquely his.

Children and adults approach grief and mourning differently. Children tend to grieve in small spurts, showing sadness only occasionally. Or their grief manifests physically as headaches or stomachaches. Grief is more stretched out over time for children, since they take in different aspects of their loss as they grow. Big events, like high school graduation, can bring on a new time of grief.

That's why it is important to have several short, ongoing discussions about the death, over time. Letting grief rise up naturally, acknowledging it, then allowing it to descend for a time helps your child to cope with her loss in her own style.

GRIEF THROUGH THE AGES

Since development and age play such an important role in how children grieve and mourn, this book is broken down into three age groups:

> Preschoolers — ages 3 to 5
> School-agers — ages 6 to 11
> Teenagers — ages 12 to 19

These groupings represent distinct developmental stages in children's lives. With that said, I do not believe children of the same age always grieve in the same way. It's important to see these age groupings as somewhat arbitrary. You may know a precocious five-year-old who is cognitively more akin to a seven-year-old or a young teen who has not yet developed the skill of abstract thinking. You know the child best, and it's your place to decide what fits for her and what doesn't. Trust your intuition and knowledge of who she is and how she operates emotionally, socially, cognitively, and spiritually and decide which category fits her best.

Researchers have studied the ways in which chronological age affects a child's response to loss. In general, these studies found that children five and under usually do not fully understand death, especially its finality. For children older than five, the studies are mixed. One found that children six and older understand that death is final, while another found that only children nine years and older do so. Factors such as familiarity with death, self-concept, and intelligence also play an important role in an individual child's understanding of death. For these reasons, defining how a child might respond to death simply by age is inaccurate. Therefore these age breakdowns are simply guidelines.

HELPING INFANTS AND TODDLERS WHEN SOMEONE THEY LOVE DIES
Due to their age, infants and toddlers demand special mention. Many adults think that because very young children are not completely aware of what is going on around them, they are not impacted by death. We must dispel this misconception. I say it simply: Any child old enough to love is old enough to mourn.

True, infants and toddlers are not developmentally mature enough to fully understand the concept of death. In fact, many children do not truly understand the inevitability and permanence of death until adolescence.

But understanding death and being affected by it are two very different things. When a primary caregiver dies, even tiny babies notice and react to the loss. They might not know exactly what happened and why, but they do know that someone important is now missing from their small worlds.

THE SPECIAL NEEDS OF GRIEVING INFANTS
As anyone who has been around infants knows, babies quickly bond with their parents and other primary caregivers. In fact, studies have shown that babies just hours old recognize and respond to their mothers' voices. Many psychologists even believe that babies think they and their mothers are one and the same person for a number of months.

This powerful and exclusive attachment to mommy and daddy continues through most of the first year of life. When a parent dies, then, there is no question the baby notices that something is missing. She will likely protest her loss by crying more than usual, sleeping more or less than she did before, or changing her eating patterns.

• **Offer comfort**
  When they are upset, most infants are soothed by physical contact. Pick up the bereaved infant

when he cries. Wear him in a front pack; he will be calmed by your heartbeat and motion. Give him a gentle baby massage. Talk to him and smile at him as much as possible.

And do not worry about spoiling him. The more you hold him, rock him, and sing to him, the more readily he will realize that though things have changed, someone will always be there to take care of him.

- **Take care of basic needs**
  Besides lots of love, an infant needs to be fed, sheltered, diapered, and bathed. Try to maintain the grieving baby's former schedule. But don't be surprised if she sleeps or eats more or less than usual. Such changes are her way of showing her grief. If she starts waking up several times a night, soothe her back to sleep. The most important thing you can do is to meet her needs—whatever they seem to be—quickly and lovingly in the weeks and months to come.

THE SPECIAL NEEDS OF GRIEVING TODDLERS

Like infants, bereaved toddlers mostly need our love and attention. They also need us to help them understand that though it is painful, grief is the price we pay for the priceless chance to love others. They need us to teach them that death is a normal and natural part of life.

- **Offer comfort and care**
  The bereaved toddler needs one-on-one care 24 hours a day. Make sure someone she loves and trusts is always there to feed her, clothe her, diaper her, and play with her. Unless she is already comfortable with a certain provider, now is not the time to put her in daycare.

  Expect regressive behaviors from grieving toddlers. Those who slept well before may now wake up during the night. Independent children may now be afraid to leave their parents' side. Formerly potty-trained kids may need diapers again. All of these behaviors are normal grief responses. They are the toddler's way of saying, "I'm upset by this death and I need to be taken care of right now." By tending to her baby-like needs, you will be letting her know that she will be taken care of and that she is loved without condition.

- **Model your own grief**
  Toddlers learn by imitation. If you mourn in healthy ways, toddlers will learn to do the same. Don't hide your feelings when you're around children. Instead, share them. Cry if you want to. Be angry if you want to. Let the toddler know that these painful feelings are not directed at him and are not his fault, however.

  Sometimes you may feel so overwhelmed by your own grief that you can't make yourself emotionally available to the bereaved toddler. You needn't feel guilty about this; it's OK to need some "alone time" to mourn. In fact, the more fully you allow yourself to do your own work of mourning, the sooner you'll be available to help the child. In the meantime, make sure other caring adults are around to nurture the grieving toddler.

- **Use simple, concrete language**

  When someone a toddler loves dies, he will know that person is missing. He may ask for Mommy or Uncle Ted one hundred times a day. I recommend using the word "dead" in response to his queries.

  Say, "Mommy is dead, honey. She can never come back." Though he won't yet know what "dead" means, he will begin to differentiate it from "bye-bye" or "gone" or "sleeping"—terms that only confuse the issue. Tell him that dead means the body stops working. The person can't walk or talk anymore, can't breathe, and can't eat. And while using simple, concrete language is important, remember that more than two-thirds of your support will be conveyed nonverbally.

- **Keep change to a minimum.**

  All toddlers need structure, but bereaved toddlers, especially, need their daily routines. Keeping mealtimes, bedtime, and bath time the same lets them know that their life continues and that they will always be cared for. And try not to implement other changes right away. Now is not the time to go from a crib to a bed, to potty train, or to wean from a bottle.

How children ages 3 to 5 typically respond to grief

Since preschool-aged children do not see a distinct line between real and imaginary, they may think of death as temporary or reversible or may equate it with sleeping. On television or video games, death is a common occurrence—often with the "dead" animal or person coming back to life! On the other hand, young children have often seen actual death up close, in the form of dead insects, wild animals, and small pets. So, death is a great mystery, and children perceive this at a young age.

Preschoolers are still building their vocabulary and their ability to communicate by expressing words. They may not understand these mixed feelings of grief, let alone know how to verbalize them. They need help naming these feelings. Preschoolers may also ask questions about the death over and over again to try to understand it. It's important to be honest and answer their questions truthfully.

Because they cannot express themselves in words easily, preschoolers may do so in play. They may reenact the death as a way of exploring their feelings and understanding of death. Don't be shocked by "death play." It's a perfectly natural way for a young child to integrate the reality of the death. Besides play, preschool children might express grief physically, as words are difficult to form for such big concepts. They might be irritable, explosive, or have "melt downs," or have a hard time sleeping. They will need extra physical comfort, as sometimes hugs and holding are better understood than words.

Also, young children are egocentric and assume they have control over what happens in their world. They may think a death is their fault. Maybe if they would have done what they were told to do or been "good," the death would not have happened. They may secretly blame themselves, causing erratic behaviors.

Finally, preschoolers, like toddlers, may regress. A child who had gained independence, like going off to preschool without separation anxiety, may lose it and become clingy. He may seek comfort in old habits that soothed him, like sucking his thumb or sleeping with his parents. He may start talking baby talk again and even revert back to needing diapers. Short-term regressive behaviors are normal and simply indicate his need for comfort.

TELLING A PRESCHOOLER SOMEONE IS DYING OR HAS DIED

YOU CAN SAY:

"Come sit on my lap. I have something to tell you. I am very sad to say this, but _____ is dying (or has died). I know you love _____ very much, but once s/he dies (or now that s/he has died), you won't be able to be with him/her anymore. When a person dies, their body stops working. They don't see, hear, feel, eat, or breathe, or move. Once the body completely stops working, it will never start working again and the person can never come back. The body has died. I know it is sad and I know you might need to cry about it, and that's OK. You can talk to me anytime you want, and you can ask any questions you want. Do you have any questions, now? Or do you need me to hold you?"

How children ages 6 to 11 typically respond to grief
School-aged children have a clearer understanding of death. For the most part, they know death is permanent and unavoidable. However, death might still carry strong imaginative connotations and children may think of the person who died as a ghost, skeleton, or angel.

Children ages 10 and 11 have a more "adult" understanding of death. However, some see death as only happening to other people, not to them or their family. When it does, they are extra shocked and rattled.

Children in this age group continue to express their grief primarily through play. They may "hang back" socially and scholastically. They may act out because they don't know how else to handle their grief feelings, especially those of anger, anxiety, shame, guilt, sadness, and worry. Children of this age can harbor fears of their own death or others with whom they are close. School-aged children, especially those younger, may still worry about who will take care of them.

TELLING A SCHOOL-AGED CHILD SOMEONE IS DYING OR HAS DIED

YOU CAN SAY:
"Come sit over here by me. I have something to tell you. I feel really sad to have to tell you this, but _____ is dying (or has died). I know you love _____ very much and it will feel hard to not have him/her in your life anymore. You will probably feel lots of feelings, like sadness, confusion, numbness, disbelief, and even anger. You might think "Why is this happening?" These thoughts and feelings are normal. I know it doesn't seem fair, but even though people don't talk about it much, death is really just a part of life. Of course, we wish it wasn't happening (or hadn't happened) to _____, but it is (did). I want you to know you can talk to me anytime you want, and ask me any questions about it. I understand this is hard for you to hear. Do you have any questions, now?"

How children ages 12 to 19 typically respond to grief
Companioning a teenager demands special care. Death for teens is complicated, as it falls at a time when developmentally they are naturally gaining independence and separating from their parents and family. Teens still need comfort and companionship through death, but they might naturally resist the seeming sense of dependence it brings. Teens often turn toward friends, rather than family, for support. Don't assume they are getting their needs met by friends alone.

Teens understand death cognitively but are only beginning to grapple with it spiritually. They are just starting to explore the "why" questions about life and death. While teens understand death, they often do not have the ability to cope with death as an adult would. Death also goes against a teenage sense of invincibility, which can make teens question their understanding of how the world works. The shaking of this foundation can feel threatening and can cause confusion and anger. Teens may protest the loss by acting out and/or withdrawing from school, friends, family, and activities that bring meaning. They may test their own mortality by taking risks.

THE SIX NEEDS OF MOURNING

1. Accept the reality of the death.

2. Let yourself feel the pain of the loss.

3. Remember the person who died.

4. Develop a new self-identity.

5. Search for meaning.

6. Let others help you—now and always.

Teenagers often feel life has been unfair to them when a death occurs. A teen's normal egocentrism can cause her to focus exclusively on the effect the death has had on her and her future. Teens can adopt a "why me?" attitude about death and become overwhelmed with feelings that they don't know how to handle.

Adolescence is naturally stressful because of the developmental tasks teens must undertake. For the bereaved teen, this combination of normal challenges and the experience of grief can potentially be overwhelming. Don't be surprised if seemingly minor stresses make the bereaved teen very upset. She might cry or get angry because her locker is stuck or she misplaced a book. Have extra patience when companioning grieving teens.

TELLING A TEENAGER SOMEONE IS DYING OR HAS DIED

YOU CAN SAY:

"Come sit over here by me. I have something to tell you. It feels unbelievable and awful that I have to tell you this, but _____ is dying (or has died). I know you love _____ very much and it will feel hard and maybe even impossible not to have him/her in your life now or in the future to watch you grow up, go to college, get a job, and start a family of your own. Over the next weeks and months you will probably feel lots of feelings, like sadness, confusion, numbness, disbelief, and even anger. You might think "Why me?" or "Why is this happening?" That is normal and natural. I know it doesn't seem fair, but even though people don't talk about it much, death is really just a part of life. Of course, we wish it wasn't happening (or hadn't happened) to _____, but it is (did). I want you to know you can talk to me anytime you want, and ask me any questions about it. I understand how difficult this must be for you to hear. Do you have any questions now?"

"Be the change that you want to see in the world."

— MAHATMA GHANDI

CHAPTER TWO

Companioning children through grief

HABITS OF A GOOD COMPANION

To companion children on a journey through grief and mourning is an important gift of healing. It takes wisdom and courage to step back and let the child lead. It is not always easy to observe a child's grief without feeling a need to pass judgment or command action. Above all, it takes patience because it is difficult to watch a child in pain without wanting to "fix it" or make it go away. The following guidelines will help you be a good companion to a child in grief.

Let him lead

When you put a child in charge of his own grief, you show respect for his loss and his unique way of processing his pain. Show up with curiosity and a willingness to bear witness to his grief in whatever form it takes, knowing that grief is a process, always changing, always moving. A good companion in grief and mourning honors the mystery without feeling a need to solve the child's grief or label it a problem that has to be overcome.

In order to let the child lead, you must become familiar with her story and how she tells it. Some children might express their grief through physical play, drawing, or pretend games. Others might express it by crying at unexpected times (called "griefbursts") or asking nonstop questions in a quest to understand it. Others will withdraw and go off on their own. However a child expresses her grief, it is her story and she is the one telling it. It's your job as her companion to observe, encourage questions, and create a safe place for her to express all her thoughts and feelings.

As a companion, you provide a nurturing, gentle environment in which the child not only heals but grows. After time and with the compassionate care of adults, grieving kids adapt to their new, sometimes hostile surroundings and go on to not just survive, but thrive. I have been privileged to witness this transformation many times. And when it happens, it is awe-inspiringly natural and beautiful, like watching a caterpillar emerge from its chrysalis as a butterfly. It is, at bottom, why I am a grief counselor.

Be an observer

A key to healing is acceptance. As a companion, giving the message that you do not have expectations of the child will allow him to express his feelings in whatever way he needs. Watch the child. Take cues from him on how to talk about the death and under what circumstances. Maybe you notice that he is especially chatty when the two of you are playing in the yard. Notice the nonverbal messages he sends when you bring up certain topics or undertake activities, like looking through photo albums. See how he copes with the death and allow room for what you don't understand.

Encourage questions

Not only is it a companion's job to explain death and describe feelings of loss, it is also your place to encourage questions. Don't be afraid that you won't be able to answer them. You don't have to have all the answers. It is OK to give a limited yet open answer and let the child know you will find out the answer (or think about the answer) and get back to her. Be a good listener and ask open-ended questions with long pauses, allowing her to form her thoughts and fill in the silence on her terms. Remember—mystery is something to be pondered, not explained.

Welcome her feelings

Children are naturally more authentic than adults. They have not integrated social norms as deeply as adults have and often act out how they feel rather than what's expected of them. Sometimes their actions are out of line of what we "expect" a person in grief should do. Maybe you worry what relatives or others might think if the child is acting "unconventionally," such as laughing and playing football after Grandpa's funeral rather than sitting on the couch looking sober. After all, other adults might read his reaction as a lack of feelings or a sign of denial or even indifference to the death. Resist the urge to place expectations on children. Instead, let their grief be expressed naturally and as they intend. Remember that children communicate in a variety of ways. Rough, physical play in itself may be an expression of grief. It might also be a needed break from the intense feelings that grieving brings.

If the child shows his grief by exploding or melting down, it's a companion's place to tolerate, encourage, and validate these explosive emotions without judging, retaliating, or arguing. It's wise to remain open and throw away preconceived ideas of what a bereaved child should look like or act like. Simply be alert to his words, moods, and reactions. Let the child teach you if explosive emotions are part of his grief experience or not. If you simply listen and watch as the child demonstrates his anger, he will come to understand that his feelings are accepted. When he calms down, you might explore, with curiosity, why he thinks he felt so angry. Remember, a key to companioning is following, not leading.

Be patient

When it comes to grief and children, loving adult companions must be patient in two ways: patient in the moments and patient over the years. Children may try your patience as they ask questions repeatedly or respond to grief in unusual ways. Since children can only cognitively understand death and grief from within the parameters of their development, it may take a long time—even years—for children to fully express their grief and move toward healing. They might literally need to grow into the ability to express their grief or understand the full extent of their loss. Letting go of your own definition of grief will allow you the patience and tolerance you need to companion them on their journeys.

Include her in ceremonies and conversations
Funerals and ceremonies are opportunities to formally mourn—to let the grief that is on the inside, out. Funerals and other death rituals are important in jumpstarting the grieving and healing process. Traditionally, there has been a habit to "protect" children from the pain of a funeral. Yet, like adults, children need the healing opportunities that funerals bring, such as making the death real, honoring the person who died with love and song, and giving an opportunity to say the first of many goodbyes. For young children especially, it makes the unreal more real. It's even OK for children to participate in the funeral or ceremony if they so desire. It lets them know their feelings matter and it's acceptable to express them.

If adults clam up when a young child enters a conversation, she gets the message that the death should not be talked about. She also thinks that if adults don't want to talk about it, it must be bad or shameful. She might even think she did something wrong to cause their discomfort. Whenever you can, include children in conversations about the death. Talk about the person who died often and tell stories of special times the child and the person who died spent together. Over time, she will understand that she is who she is partly because of the role that person played in her life and she will integrate cherished memories.

FINDING THE RIGHT WORDS—GUIDELINES ON HOW TO TALK TO GRIEVING CHILDREN

Through the years I have learned a great deal from many grieving children and their families. They have taught me which words work best when talking to children about death. While this book provides suggested language for specific situations, here are some general concepts I suggest companions use when talking with children about death, dying, grief, and mourning.

Talk openly about death

The child's journey through grief depends on you being honest and open about the death he has experienced. You may feel that if you are quiet and don't talk about it, you are helping him forget about the death and not be reminded of the pain it brings. Yet this kind of protection doesn't help for too long. Of course you mean well, but by not talking about the death, which is foremost on everyone's minds, you only cause him to feel confused and alone in his grief. It might even make him feel more afraid.

When talking with children, use simple, concrete language. Until they become teenagers, children are quite literal. Try not to use abstract or complex descriptions for death. It's OK to use the "d" word (death or dying). Explain death in a straightforward manner, without the use of metaphors or analogies such as "passed away," "taking a long sleep," "left us," or "in a better place." Be open to discussing the death and his thoughts and feelings about it again and again. That's because healing is a process, not an event.

WHEN THEY ASK: *"What is death?"*

YOU CAN SAY: *"When people die, their bodies stop working. They don't see, hear, feel, eat, or breathe anymore. Once the body completely stops working, it will never start working again and the person can never come back."*

Share your feelings
A natural part of healing is seeing that others feel the same way
that you do. Let the child see you grieving and mourning. Don't
be afraid of scaring her by letting her see you cry. Remember,
crying is really an act of strength, not weakness. Crying together
is healing. It allows you to express your grief in a raw and honest
way. By grieving together you send the strong message that she is
not alone in her grief.

> **WHEN THEY SAY:**   *"I wish Nana was here."*
>
> **YOU CAN SAY:**   *"Me too. It makes my heart ache to think we
> won't ever see her here with us again."*

Be honest and direct
Answer questions simply and directly. Adults may think they
need to explain everything, but young children are often satisfied
with an honest, short answer. For example, just the first two
sentences of this explanation would suffice: "I think it is sad that
Grandpa died. What do you think? Yet Grandpa had a long and
happy life. Some people are not ready to die because they haven't
done enough, but Grandpa did so much. Did you know he was in
World War II? Anyway, he was blessed with so much. Much more
than most people, so in a way I think he was ready to die...."

> **WHEN THEY SAY:**   *"Did it hurt Sam when he died?"*
>
> **YOU CAN SAY:**   *"When our bodies experience trauma—a big
> hit or shock—they release chemicals that
> block our bodies from feeling pain. This
> probably happened when the car hit Sam,
> so no, I don't think it hurt."*

Avoid euphemisms

Saying a dead person is "asleep," for example, will not only mislead a child, it may also cause her to believe that the dead person might "wake up" again. Or if you say, "It was God's will," she might feel angry at God for taking her mother, sister, or friend away from her. Or she might believe that God is punishing her. I also caution people about the phrase "passed away." While that often has theological connotations related to your belief system, for young children this can be confusing. I recommend using the words "dead" and "died." Other common euphemisms are: "passed on," "kicked the bucket," "gone to your reward," "went West," or "there has been a celestial discharge." Remember, young children take things literally, so such abstractions are often confusing. Also, keep in mind that children can cope with what they know. They cannot cope with what they don't know or have been "protected" from knowing.

WHEN THEY SAY:	*"What happened to Grandpa?"*
DON'T SAY:	*"Grandpa expired." or "Grandpa passed away."*
YOU CAN SAY:	*"Grandpa died."*

Teach what you believe

When you talk to children about death, the conversation will often naturally head toward the topic of what happens after death. The key is to teach what you believe. If you believe in an afterlife, tell the child about your understanding of heaven, always using simple, age-appropriate language. If you do not believe in an afterlife, it's OK to tell her that you believe that life is a gift that happens here on Earth and when life ends, what remains are our precious memories. And don't forget to ask her what *she* thinks happens after death. You might be surprised that she has already developed a detailed and comforting belief.

> **WHEN THEY SAY:** *"Will Grandpa be able to see Grandma now that he is in heaven?"*
>
> **YOU CAN SAY:** *"While I don't know for sure, I think that is what it is like. That's what I believe."* *(If you believe this.)*

Give inviting, loving nonverbal cues

For children, the language of comfort is often physical—through holding, hugging, snuggling, and affection. Spend time simply sitting next to or holding the child. Your close physical presence is a conversation in itself.

When talking about the death or the child's grief, stay aware of your tone and make eye contact. With warmth, sincerity, and a relaxed open face, send the message that whatever she says is OK, allowing her to express her fears and wishes freely. Allow long pauses after questions or gaps in talking for her to fill or not.

Sometimes it's easier for older children to talk without direct eye contact or while doing something else, such as riding in the car, walking together, cooking, or doing another activity together. Create ample opportunities for these casual, inviting situations.

It's also important to honor how children best express themselves— and sometimes that's not through talking. Maybe it's drawing, writing in a journal, singing loudly, roughhousing, dancing, doing crafts, watching videos, or looking through pictures to remember the person who died. Tune in to the child's personality and create opportunities for various ways for her to express her grief.

> **WHEN THEY SAY:** *"I miss Uncle Matt."*
>
> **YOU CAN SAY:** *"I miss him too. How about we write him a letter and tell him how you feel? Or I can help you create a memory box of things that*

> *remind you of him, or we can listen to his*
> *favorite band and look at photos of us and*
> *Uncle Matt. It will be like a little visit with him.*
> *Does that sound good to you?"*

Attend to your own grief

If you are a parent or family member, most likely you are also
grieving the death of the person who died. When you are
overwhelmed by death, it's hard to think of anything else,
including the needs of those around you.

It's important for you to carve out time and honor your own grief.
If you are responsible for the fulltime care of a child, you will
have to do the same for her—creating time for her to grieve with
you and separately. Giving attention to another's grief can be
challenging when grief has shaken you deeply, but try your best to
be available to your child, who feels shocked and confused by the
death of a family member or a loved one. If, understandably, you
just can't do it right now, find another loving adult who can.

Your child needs full-on love and attention right now—at a time
when it might feel the hardest to give. Remember that your
grief may look very different than her grief. While you may be
overwhelmed with sadness, her feelings may be more muddled
and undefined. She may be able to digest just a little of her grief at
a time before needing a mental and emotional break, while your
grief may be all-consuming.

It's important to ask for help from friends and family; let them
take on some of the responsibility of companioning your child
through her grief. The task may even be too large for you and
your circle of friends and family to handle. If so, that's OK. Enlist a
professional counselor or seek the help of grief support groups as
needed. Mostly, be gentle with yourself and know you are doing
the best you can.

"We're taught to expect unconditional love from our parents, but I think it is more the gift our children give us. It's they who love us helplessly, no matter what or who we are."

— KATHRYN HARRISON

CHAPTER THREE

When a parent dies

The loss of a parent is typically the greatest pain of all for children. Parents are a child's sturdy ground, and much of what they know and experience has been built up from this foundation. Nearly every thought, action, or idea a young child experiences first passes through the filter of how his parents perceive, respond, and act in the world. Since the lives of child and parent are so intertwined, losing a parent feels to a child like losing a part of himself. It can leave him feeling lost and confused and unsure of how to proceed with his life without the parent there to guide him. He can feel anxiety and fear without the constant force of the parent in his life. Preschoolers, especially, need constant reassurance that you are there to care for them.

PRESCHOOLERS—AGES 3 TO 5
Talking to preschoolers about a parent's death

WHEN THEY SAY: *"Where is mommy? When will she come home?"*

DON'T SAY: *"She is up in the sky wearing angel wings and flying around happily."*

           OR:

           "She is in a better place. But we are here to take care of you and love you."

SAY: *"Mommy is dead. She can never come back. But we are here to take care of you and love you."*

BECAUSE: Even though it is hard to hear, your preschooler must understand that her mother is gone forever. Until she understands, she will live in limbo waiting for her mother to walk through the door. Metaphorical or philosophical answers will not be understood by preschoolers. They only complicate the issue of death and further confuse her understanding of real versus imaginary. She might think, "If she has wings, why doesn't she fly down and see me?" or "Why does she want to be there instead of here with me? Did I make this a bad place by being bad?" She may ask you several times about death. That's because young children can think death is different for different living things or that death has degrees. For example, I once worked with a boy who said bugs and people were a "different kind of dead." He believed people could come back to life if given food, but bugs couldn't.

WHEN THEY SAY: *"Will you die, too, Daddy?"*

DON'T SAY: *"Of course, everybody dies."*

SAY: *"All of us want to live for a long, long time. That is what I plan to do. I will be around longer than you can even imagine. I will be here to take care of you."*

BECAUSE: What a young child probably wants to know

is, "Will you take care of me now that Mommy is gone?" Preschoolers often worry about who will be responsible for them, as they depend so strongly on a parent's care. The world is a scary place without a dedicated adult, and they need reassurance that you, or someone else, will care for them.

WHEN THEY SAY: *"Why did Mommy go away? She's mean!"*

DON'T SAY: *"Don't be mad at Mommy! She was a good mommy who loved you very much!"*

SAY: *"Mommy loved you very much. She didn't want to die and leave you. It wasn't anyone's fault. I am here to take care of you, and I will not leave you."*

BECAUSE: Your child feels abandoned and misses the care and love from his mother. With anger, he is protesting the death of his mother and expressing his grief over her absence. He may not understand that death is not a choice. Respond to the hurt with reassurance that his mother didn't leave him on purpose and that you are here to care for him. If you respond angrily to his anger, you might instill feelings of guilt or shame.

WHEN THEY SAY: *"I miss Mommy."*

DON'T SAY: *"Don't worry about Mommy. Mommy is happy in heaven."*

SAY: *"I do too, sweetie. Mommy was a great mommy. You miss her because you loved her very much, and she loved you."*

BECAUSE: If you respond with false resolve, your child will feel confused by her grief feelings of sadness and wonder if she is wrong to have them. Trying to ease her pain or worry by pretending to have feelings you don't have, or clinging to ideas that you don't really believe, will only heighten her pain. She will feel alone in her missing, and she might think she shouldn't express her sadness over her mother's death. Instead, empathize with her, letting her know you also share her sadness and deep grief.

WHEN THEY SAY: *"You don't do it like Mommy did! I want Mommy!"*

DON'T SAY: *"Mommy is gone and I am in charge now."*

SAY: *"I miss Mommy too. Come over here and show me the way you want me to do it."*

BECAUSE: When a parent dies, a child's life is completely disrupted, including routines. Preschoolers will feel grief around concrete things that have changed. He might seemingly overreact to small things, like the way you button his coat (since it's different than how mom did it) or driving him to preschool (because that's when he and mom talked the most). These moments are painful reminders of his loss. See these strong reactions over little things as grief expressed and respond with compassion.

WHEN THEY SAY: *"If Mommy comes home I will be good."*

DON'T SAY: *"Yes, Mommy would want you to be good."*

SAY: *"Mommy didn't leave because you were being bad, honey. It doesn't matter if you act good or bad, it won't bring her back. Mommy died, and when people die, they can't come back to life. Ever. We just have to figure out together how to live without her. I know it's hard now, but someday it will get better."*

BECAUSE: The young child irrationally might believe that her mom "left" because she was bad or did things her mother didn't like. Alternatively, she may act out and "be bad," believing that if she is bad enough, Mom will have to come back to punish her. This is especially true if the parent who died was the main disciplinarian in the house.

SCHOOL-AGERS—AGES 6 TO 11
Talking to school-aged kids about a parent's death

WHEN THEY SAY: *"Why did Mom have to die?"*

DON'T SAY: *"Because it was God's will."*
OR:
"Because heaven needed another angel."

SAY: *"We all die someday. We all hope to live until we are old, but sometimes that doesn't happen. If Mom had the choice, she would still be with us."*
OR:
"It is no one's fault that Mom died. No one gets a choice about when they die. I know it doesn't feel fair and that you miss her."

BECAUSE: Most school-aged children have not formed a sense of spirituality and still often view the idea of God as literal—a great man in the sky. Because of this, they may feel mad at God and confused, especially if they have learned through the sharing of religious beliefs or through religious education that God is good and that God equals love. They may think, "How could a loving God do this to me? God must not like me very much." What they really need is acknowledgment of their grief.

WHEN THEY SAY: *"Let's play house. I will be the mom. I am going to die."*

DON'T SAY: *"That's terrible! It's bad enough that Mom died. Don't make it worse!"*
OR:
"That's not appropriate!"

SAY: *"OK, let's. I will be the dad and you be the mom."*

BECAUSE: While death play can strike adults as morbid and crude, it is an essential way for younger children to process the profound experience. Remember, school-aged kids know that death is permanent, but they don't understand the reason death happens or the spiritual aspects of death. They have a lot of questions and understanding to gain. Acting out the death allows them to express their feelings at a safe distance, as well as work out what death means. See it as an opportunity to interject healthy views of death, dying, grief, and mourning, and to also get a chance to see what beliefs or feelings—like guilt or fear—the child might be harboring.

WHEN THEY SAY: *"Now that mom is gone, who will take me shopping, drive me to dance class, fix my hair, etc., etc.?"*

DON'T SAY: *"You will have to grow up and figure out some of those things on your own."*

SAY: *"Don't worry. We will figure it out together."*
OR:
"We can always call Aunt Mary (or Sophie's mom, or Grandma Smith...) and she will help."

BECAUSE: School-aged kids (and preschoolers) learn a lot about their gender by mimicking their same-sex parent. Whether it is mom or dad who died, you can help identify someone close of that gender to step in as a "model" for the child through the upcoming years.

WHEN THEY SAY: *"I wish you would have died instead!"*

DON'T SAY: *"That's it! Go to your room. You're grounded!"*
OR:
"Well, too bad. You are stuck with me."

OR:
"You are mean. I wish you would learn to be nicer."

SAY: *"I know that you are angry right now, and that you don't mean that. I'll give you some time to calm down and then if you want to talk, we can."*

OR:
"You are mad that Mom is gone. I understand. I wish she was here, too. But I am here for you, and I always will be."

BECAUSE: The child is expressing his grief with anger and wants to blame someone for the death or make someone pay. While this is not pleasant to experience, do your best to step out of the situation and see it for what it is. He is in pain. He misses his mother. If he is a boy, he may think he should be "strong" and a "man" and that he shouldn't cry, so his pent-up grief turns to anger. Respond with love and encourage softer emotions of sadness and sorrow to come forth. Let him know it is OK to cry, that it's what humans do when someone they love has died.

WHEN THEY SAY: *"No! Mom isn't really gone. I just know it!"*

DON'T SAY: *"We just have to accept it and continue on with our lives."*

SAY: *"I know it is hard to believe. You don't have to accept it until you are ready, but I don't want you to get stuck in hopes that mom will come back. She can't, honey, no matter how hard you wish for it."*

BECAUSE: The child is not ready to accept the death and the fact that her mother will never return. The pain of this realization is too great. Watch for denial: a complete refusal to talk about the person, avoiding spending time at home, etc. It's OK if this goes on for a short time, but if you notice that she is holding on to a fantasy ("Mom's just on a trip; she'll be back.") or it is interfering with her relationships, she needs help. Encourage her to talk about her loss. Help her find a trusted adult, if it's not you. Go to the library and help her check out books on grief. Research support groups in your area. She must move beyond this denial to heal. I have worked with many adults who suffer from unreconciled grief from their youth.

SEEKING HELP FOR COMPLICATED MOURNING

Here are signs of complicated mourning—indicating that a child or teen would benefit from professional help. Think of complicated mourning as normal mourning with the volume turned way up. While all these signs are a normal part of mourning, the difference is the child tends to get stuck in them, and they become chronic and prolonged, without relief. With normal mourning, the child passes through waves of each of these (maybe over and over again), but doesn't experience them forever.

- Total denial of the death
- Persistent panic and fear
- Unresolved physical complaints
- Lingering feelings of guilt or responsibility for the death
- Chronic apathy and depression
- Chronic hostility
- Long-term change in behaviors and personality
- Consistent withdrawal from friends and family
- Dramatic, ongoing changes in sleeping and eating
- Drug or alcohol abuse
- Suicidal thoughts or actions

TEENAGERS—AGES 12 TO 19
Talking to teenagers about a parent's death

WHEN THEY SAY: *"Why me? Why did my mother have to die?"*

DON'T SAY: *"It's just the way it is. The sooner you accept it, the better."*

SAY: *"I don't have a good answer for that. I know that doesn't help and that you feel singled out. I do know that there are other teens who have lost a parent. In fact, there is a support group in town just for kids your age. Do you want me to take you there?"*
OR:
"Oh honey, it is nothing you did or any of us did. It has to feel really hard to live every day without her. What's that like for you?"

BECAUSE: She is feeling victimized by the death of her mother. The death came at a time when her life may already be overwhelming. Many teenagers feel immense social and academic pressure, along with the increasing stress of needing to "grow up" and be independent. Teens are no longer children, yet they are not adults yet either. Losing a parent during this time can be particularly devastating. Mostly, she needs love, understanding, and support. Let her know she is not alone in her grief. Ask her open-ended questions to encourage discussions and help her tap into the resources of the community at large.

WHEN THEY SAY: *"Life isn't worth living if Mom isn't around!"*

DON'T SAY: *"Of course it is. Your mother didn't want to die. Life is a gift."*
OR:

"You must not think that way. You have to live the best life ever for your mother."

SAY: *"You really seem to be hurting. Let's find you someone to talk with about it."*

OR:

"Tell me more about that. I know it's hard."

BECAUSE: Grieving can be especially difficult for teenagers. Toying with the idea of suicide is a sign that he needs extra help. So are symptoms of depression, sleeping problems, and an indifference to school, activities, or friends. He may also act out his pain through risky behaviors. It's time to seek outside help from a school counselor, support group, therapist, or other resources in your community. Also, take such statements as signs that you need to give extra time and attention to the teen, and really listen when he talks about his pain. There's a chance he is merely crying out for help and simply needs to be heard—and for someone to acknowledge his pain. But it needs to be assessed.

WHEN THEY SAY: *"You don't understand what I am going through."*

DON'T SAY: *"Of course I do. I lost her too!"*

SAY: *"You're right. Your grief is unique to you, and my grief is unique to me. It makes me feel _____. Will you tell me how it is for you?"*

BECAUSE: Teens may think they need to be "mature and grown up" and not show emotions or feel flattened by grief. They may try to push you away. Let them know that expressing their feelings with tears or anguish is a normal part of mourning, at any age. Witness for them what it looks like to mourn. Don't hide your own grief. Share it with them.

WHEN THEY SAY: *"Just leave me alone."*

DON'T SAY: *"Fine. I will."*

SAY: *"It sounds like you don't want to talk right now. Just know I am here if you change your mind. It's good to talk about it. Is there someone else you'd like to talk to about it?"*

BECAUSE: As teens strive for independence, they may push family members away. This is a normal part of their real need to separate from you. Don't take it personally. They are simply trying to form an identity separate from you or the family. Yet there is still a real need to talk out her personal experience of what it is like to lose her parent. Yet be aware that grieving teens often seek alone time and honor that—as long as she isn't isolating herself all the time.

WHEN THEY SAY: *"I miss Mom."*

DON'T SAY: *"You are almost an adult now. You have to be strong and help your dad."*
OR:
"Don't worry. You will learn to carry on without her."
OR:
"I know, but you have to get on with your life. Your mother would have wanted it that way."

SAY: *"I know. I miss her so much too. What do you need? Is there anything I can do to help?"*
OR:
"Losing a parent is really hard, and I know Mom was super important to you. Just know that it's OK to cry, wail, yell, run around, scream, and do whatever you need to get your feelings out. It's your grief and yours alone to express. There are no rules about how

you should grieve or how long it should take."

BECAUSE: Even though your teen might look like an adult,
he is still a child. Teens are usually expected to
be "grown up" and support other members of
the family, particularly a surviving parent or
younger brothers and sisters. Many teens have
been told, "Now you will have to take care of your
family." The problem is this: When a teenager
feels responsible for "taking care of the family," he
doesn't have the opportunity, or the permission,
to mourn. Foster his grief and encourage his
mourning to come forth—in whatever form. Don't
assume he will find comfort in his friends. Let him
know that you are there for him no matter what
he needs—and that you understand that this is a
difficult time for him. Treat him with extra care.

"Brothers and sisters are as close as hands and feet."

— A VIETNAMESE PROVERB

CHAPTER FOUR

When a sibling dies

Besides the death of a parent, the death of a sibling is one of the most traumatic death experiences for children. That's because siblings often have strong feelings for each other—feelings of love and caring as well as ambivalent feelings of, say, jealousy and competition. Ambivalent feelings complicate grief and open the door to hard emotions such as guilt and self-blame. Through my experience counseling hundreds of bereaved siblings, I have found that siblings often feel four ambivalent emotions when a brother or sister dies: guilt, relief, fear, and confusion. Finally, siblings can be "forgotten mourners," as much of the support from friends and family is focused on the parents. Caring adults who are companioning a child through grief should keep this in mind.

PRESCHOOLERS—AGES 3 TO 5
Talking to preschoolers about a sibling's death

WHEN THEY SAY: *"I told Sammy I wished he was dead, and now he's dead!"*

DON'T SAY: *"Why would you wish such a thing?"*

SAY: *"Oh, sweetie. Wishes and words don't cause people to die. It's not your fault."*

BECAUSE: Preschoolers can have "magical thinking," which enables them to believe that thoughts can cause actions. Developmentally, preschoolers are egocentric and think the world revolves around them, which sometimes leads them to believe their thoughts are all-powerful. The child may feel guilty about the mixed feelings he harbored for his sister and secretly feel shame for hurting her. Even if a preschooler never says such a thing, it's wise to have a discussion about how death is no one's fault (usually). While you are at it, introduce the idea that people can sometimes have mixed feelings for each other and that doesn't mean they don't love each other.

WHEN THEY SAY: *"Sammy died, so will I die too?"*

DON'T SAY: *"Why would you ask such a thing?"*

SAY: *"No. You can't catch death like you catch a cold. Sammy was a separate person from you."*
OR:
"No. Usually people don't die until they are old. It is sad that Sammy died, but you don't have to worry about dying."

BECAUSE: Preschoolers sometimes think death is catchy, so it's good to explain that it isn't. Remember how small a young child's world is. If someone so close to her in age and in the family could die, it seems a very real possibility that she could die too. She may also carry a fear that others in the family might die. Reassure her that you and her other siblings will be around for a long time and that you will take care of her.

WHEN THEY SAY:	*"When will Sammy come home?"*
DON'T SAY:	*"Sammy is on a long trip."*
	OR:
	"Sammy is playing on the monkey bars up in heaven."
SAY:	*"Sammy can never come home. Sammy's dead. When someone dies they never come back to life."*
BECAUSE:	It's best to be direct when talking about death instead of using euphemisms that seem easier to swallow but really just confuse the child. He needs to know that his brother is never coming back so he can step into his grief and begin experiencing his feelings. While it's tempting to protect a young child by laying out a fantasy, children of all ages need to see death as a natural, albeit difficult, part of living.

WHEN THEY SAY:	*"I'm glad Sammy died!"*
DON'T SAY:	*"Shame on you!"*
SAY:	*"Why?"*
	OR:
	"Why are you glad he is gone?"
BECAUSE:	A preschooler might feel relief that her sibling—her main competitor—is gone. Now she gets more of your attention, and there is no one to take her toys. It doesn't mean that she didn't love her brother or that at other times she doesn't miss him and want him back. By asking why, you open the door for her to tell you her feelings. Resist any urge to shame her and accept that this is her feeling in the moment, and the moment will change.

SCHOOL-AGERS—AGES 6 TO 11
Talking to school-aged children about a sibling's death

WHEN THEY SAY:　*"You wish I died instead of Sam!"*

DON'T SAY:　*"Sometimes you are a difficult child and I don't always understand you."*

SAY:　*"Of course I don't. I love you both equally. I am so glad you are still alive."*
AND:
"I love Sam and I miss him, but I love you just as much."

BECAUSE:　The child might be harboring jealous feelings about Sam, thinking that you loved him more because you miss him so much. What he really needs is reassurance from you that you love him. Maybe in your own grief you haven't paid him as much attention as you could have. That's understandable, but take this question as a cue to show your love and affection.

WHEN THEY SAY:　*"Am I still a big sister?"*

DON'T SAY:　*"No, not anymore."*

SAY:　*"Even though Sam died, you will always be his big sister."*

BECAUSE:　The child is struggling with the confusing task of redefining herself now that her brother is gone. When a death happens in the immediate family, children must reestablish who they are within the family and who they are in the world at large. The child often needs direct reassurance that while her sibling has died, she is still a big sister.

WHEN THEY SAY: *"I feel bad because a part of me is glad he is gone."*

DON'T SAY: *"That's not very nice. He was a good brother to you."*

SAY: *"I understand why you would say that because I remember with my brother and sister, sometimes we would have a great time together and other times we could really fight."*

OR:

"That sounds confusing. I am sure in some ways it is easier that he's gone, like now you have your own room. But at the same time I bet you miss him when you want to play a game or ride your bike to the park."

BECAUSE: As I said, children often have conflicting feelings when it comes to the death of a sibling. It's important to acknowledge this and relieve any guilt the child might be harboring. As always, try to tap into his feelings of grief by gently asking questions about times he misses his brother. Likewise, reassure him that mixed feelings are OK and that doesn't mean he wanted his brother to die.

WHEN THEY SAY: *"I wasn't always nice to Sam."*

DON'T SAY: *"Well, I bet you wish you were nicer to him now that he is gone!"*

SAY: *"Do you remember the time when you did (such and such) for Sam? And he made you that card that said you were the (best brother in the world)?"*

OR:

"I remember that you were nice to Sam. I know you fought sometimes but that's what siblings do. Sam loved you very much."

BECAUSE: It is likely that with the above question, the child
is expressing feelings of guilt. Reassure him by
telling him that grief can bring on feelings of hurt
and confusion, and that these feelings won't last
forever.

RECOGNIZING "GRIEFBURSTS"

You might witness the child having a "griefburst." Griefbursts are sudden, strong outbursts of sadness that can happen at unexpected times and in unexpected places. Maybe your daughter is playing soccer and suddenly you see her crying on the field because she just looked for her brother on the sidelines and realized he wasn't there. Griefbursts can be extremely frightening for children. Recognize her sudden pain and provide immediate comfort.

TEENAGERS—AGES 12 TO 19
Talking to teenagers about a sibling's death

WHEN THEY SAY: *"It should have been me who died, not Sam."*
OR:
"Sam was a better person than me."

DON'T SAY: *"Don't feel that way. That's silly."*

SAY: *"Why do you say that?"*
OR:
"Each person's life is precious. You are just as worthy of life as Sam was. What are you feeling?"

BECAUSE: "Survivor guilt" is a real phenomenon. The teen might have always compared herself to her brother and fell short, thinking that he was more worthy of living than she is. She may also be idolizing him, a common occurrence after a death in which people just remember the good characteristics of a person. Or, she might feel some responsibility for the death and is looking for a way to redeem herself. Possibly, she feels guilty when she has fun and thinks, "Sam can never have fun again," or "How can I have fun when Sam died?", causing her to feel guilty that she survived and he did not.

WHEN THEY SAY: *"Life isn't fair! No one else's brother had to die."*

DON'T SAY: *"Stop feeling sorry for yourself."*
OR:
"It's time to pull up your bootstraps and move on. Sam wouldn't have wanted you to feel bad."

SAY: *"It's true. Life isn't always fair and that's hard to realize."*
OR:
"I know you feel terrible that Sam died. Even though

you don't know anyone whose brother died, it does happen, but I know it's not easy. Do you want to talk about it?"

BECAUSE: The teen is expressing both a feeling of regret over the death of his brother and also "terminal uniqueness" among his peers. Teens are highly influenced by their peers and are forever comparing themselves and their families to others. He may not be enjoying the extra attention the death brings. No teen likes to feel different or be a member of a family where bad/hard things happen. Also, the teen might be feeling victimized. When people feel victimized, they feel like they have been wronged. Empathize with the teen and let him know he is not alone in his grief.

WHEN THEY SAY: *"It feels like God is punishing me with Sam's death."*

DON'T SAY: *"Where did you ever get such an idea?"*

SAY: *"I don't think God works like that. I don't believe in a punishing God who controls our lives as if we were puppets. What do you think?"*

OR:

"Death is hard and confusing, but I don't think it happens for some greater reason. How death happens is pretty random, I think. What do you think?"

OR:

"Why do you feel like God would want to punish you? Do you think you did something wrong or that you are inherently bad for some reason?"

BECAUSE: For whatever reason, the teen is feeling guilt and thinks she is to blame for Sam's death. This might simply stem from the naturally ambivalent feelings siblings often have for each other. Or the teen may be harboring a negative belief about herself that has resulted in low self-esteem and needs to be addressed by you or a therapist. She might also be reviewing all the times she was unkind to Sam and feeling like she deserves punishment.

WHEN THEY SAY: *"I am sick of thinking about Sam. I just want to have fun for a change!"*

DON'T SAY: *"That's being disrespectful of Sam. Please don't talk that way."*

SAY: *"It sounds like you need a break from your grief and that's understandable. It can get really overwhelming to always feel that intense pain. Why don't you plan something fun with your friends, letting them know you just need to laugh for a while?"*

BECAUSE: Teens mourn in doses. That means they show signs of grief for a while then seem happy and even sometimes "uncaring" of their sibling's death. The teen needs permission to not always be openly mourning. He needs a "time-out" from his grief.

WHEN THEY SAY: *"Go away! I can handle this on my own!"*

DON'T SAY: *"Well, if that's what you want. I won't bring it up anymore."*

SAY: *"It sounds like you need some time alone right now. That's fine. If you ever want to talk, you know I am here for you, no matter what."*

BECAUSE: Teens look like adults and want to be independent, but no one, especially a young person, should cope with grief alone. Even if she pushes you away

now, she will most likely welcome and need your
support later. Accept her inconsistent signals
and know her grief and needs are ever-changing.
Her mourning might also be complicated by her
need to separate from the family, and she may
see mourning as a statement that says she "needs
you." Needing someone is incongruent with a
teen's developmental need for autonomy. Let her
know you are there if and when she changes her
mind and that grieving is not a sign of weakness
but instead a natural—and necessary—response to
death.

> *"Other things may change us, but we
> start and end with the family."*

— ANTHONY BRANDT

CHAPTER FIVE

When a grandparent dies

The degree to which a child actively grieves and mourns a
grandparent's death depends on how connected they were.
In some cases, a grandparent takes on a primary or secondary
parenting role. In others, the relationship is long distance and
visits are rare. If the grandparent was a strong matriarch or
patriarch, there can be a ripple effect across generations, because
the grandparent helped define the family and now a new family
definition must be found. It's important to let the child teach
you what the relationship was like and how much she misses
and mourns the grandparent. Never assume you know the
significance of the loss for the child.

PRESCHOOLERS—AGES 3 TO 5
Talking to preschoolers about a grandparent's death

WHEN THEY SAY: *"I wish Grandma was here."*

DON'T SAY: *"She was old and lived a great life. It was her time
to die."*

SAY: *"I do too. I miss her. Even though she was old and she lived a happy life, I am sad that she is gone. Do you miss snuggling with her?"*

BECAUSE: It is tempting to dismiss a grandparent's death because she was old and had the chance to live a long life before she died. This fact doesn't turn off or reconcile feelings of grief. We still grieve and mourn the person who died. Even under the best circumstances, death is hard and confusing. Encourage the child to tell you about his grief experience.

WHEN THEY SAY: *"Will I die like Grandma?"*

DON'T SAY: *"Grandma was sick, so she died."*

SAY: *"Yes. We all die. Every living thing dies, but people usually live a long, long time. You are young and still have to grow old before you die."*

BECAUSE: Tying death to illness might make a preschooler afraid that every time he gets sick, he might die. He might also worry every time a family member gets sick. Explain that people get sick all the time and that most of the time they feel better again, but that sometimes, when we are old and our body is worn out, we can't fight the sickness and we die.

WHEN THEY SAY: *"I want Grandma!"*

DON'T SAY: *"How about we go to the park to take away your sad feelings?"*

SAY: *"Oh, sweetie, I miss her too. Come over here and sit on my lap and we can have a cry over Grandma."*

BECAUSE: The preschooler is expressing her grief over Grandma no longer being in her life. Honor that.

Teach her that feeling emotions and crying are OK, and that's what people do when they are sad. She will learn this healthy life lesson rather than the opposite one, which teaches us to avoid hard emotions by filling the space with fun and entertainment instead. Seeing you cry along with her is cathartic and lets her know she is not alone in her grief.

WHEN THEY SAY: *"I miss Grandma."*

DON'T SAY: *"All the missing in the world won't bring her back."*

SAY: *"How about you draw me a picture of you and Grandma or make a painting about what it feels like to have Grandma gone?"*

BECAUSE: Young children do not always have the words to express their grief. Drawing and painting lets kids who are not very verbal tell a story about the death and how they feel about it. Tell him he can draw anything he likes, and give open-ended encouragement, like: "It's fun to watch you draw." You may find, as I have, that bereaved children try to compensate for their feelings of helplessness in their drawings by making powerful figures.

FIVE FACES TECHNIQUE

To foster a discussion about feelings with a preschooler, draw five faces depicting different feelings, like sadness, anger, happiness, fear, and worry. Ask him what feelings he sees in the faces. Start a conversation that explores the different feelings without judgment about good or bad feelings—letting him know that people feel all kinds of feelings, and that all feelings are OK. Ask him about times when he had such feelings, and tell him about times you had the same feelings.

SCHOOL-AGERS—AGES 6 TO 11
Talking to school-aged children about a grandparent's death

WHEN THEY SAY: *"I want to see pictures of Grandma."*

DON'T SAY: *"Let's not. It is too hard to look at them. It only makes me sad."*

SAY: *"OK. I will get the photo album and meet you on the couch."*

BECAUSE: In our grief-avoidant society, we are encouraged to remove any reminders of the person who died. Seeing pictures, watching old videos, and holding onto the person's clothing or belongings is viewed as unhealthy. Well-intentioned people may encourage you to get rid of these reminders quickly. Don't listen. Instead, view these items often and think of them as a passageway toward healing and a means to integrate your loss. Your child naturally knows this and feels the urge to "be" with Grandma when she misses her. Respect her wishes and fight the urge to turn away. It will benefit both of you. Consider which of these "linking objects" you can give to the child, such as pictures, jewelry, paintings, etc. These items will help her grief feelings surface and allow her to sort through them, as well as serve as a pleasant reminder of Grandma and their relationship.

WHEN THEY SAY: *"I wish I would have visited Grandma more often."*

DON'T SAY: *"I think you visited her enough."*

SAY: *"Sometimes after someone we love dies, we do wish we could have spent more time with her. I'm so glad Grandma knew how very much you loved her."*

BECAUSE: Statements that start with "If only..." or "I wish

I could have..." or "Why didn't I..." indicate that
the child is feeling guilt. Feeling guilt makes him
feel helpless and worthless. He may believe he
is a bad person for something he did or didn't
do when Grandma was alive. He may even
think he somehow caused Grandma's death by
disappointing her. With this sense of helplessness,
the child tries to gain a sense of control by thinking
about what he could have done differently or
punishing himself through risky behaviors. Try
to flush out, with gentle questions, what the guilt
feelings are about and help integrate them.

WHEN THEY SAY:	*"Why couldn't the doctors stop Grandma from dying?"*
DON'T SAY:	*"I think Grandma had a bad doctor. I don't think he knew what he was doing."*
SAY:	*"Many times doctors save people from dying, but sometimes they try their best and the person still dies. Their body is just too broken to fix, like Grandma's. Most people go to hospitals to get better, but once in a while, people die."*
BECAUSE:	If a child watches someone they love die in a hospital, she might form a belief that hospitals are bad places and that doctors and nurses should be avoided. It's important to reinforce that even doctors can't always control if someone will die or not, and that death is a part of life.

WHEN THEY SAY:	*"Did Grandma die because she was unhappy?"*
DON'T SAY:	*"Maybe. She was ready to die."*
SAY:	*"It seemed like Grandma was unhappy because she was in a lot of pain. When our bodies hurt really*

*badly, it's hard to smile. She also took medicines that
made her drowsy and sleepy. But she didn't die
because she was unhappy."*

BECAUSE: Children, especially younger ones, can take on
funny fears, like being unhappy or grumpy creates
a poison that kills you, or that death is catchy.
Reassure him that death is most often caused
because a body part stops working, and that body
parts usually work well our whole lives but start
breaking down, like an old car, when we get old.

WHEN THEY SAY: *"Will I ever see Grandma again?"*

DON'T SAY: *"You know Grandma is dead. Why do you ask that?"*

SAY: *"When someone dies, they can't come back alive.
I know that makes you sad."*
OR:
*"Grandma's body is buried in the ground and her
spirit is in heaven. The spirit is the part of us that
never wears out and goes on living, even after our
bodies die. Mom and Dad believe that after we die,
our spirits, or souls, leave our bodies and rise into
heaven. Faith is believing in something we can't see
but we trust is there. Because of this faith, I do think
that after you die you will see Grandma again, in
heaven."*

BECAUSE: The child probably knows death is permanent but
has a desire to see Grandma again. Acknowledge
his longing and support his feelings of sadness by
welcoming him to talk about his disappointment
over never seeing Grandma again or having to wait
until he himself dies to see Grandma in heaven.

TEENAGERS—AGES 12 TO 19
Talking to teenaged children about a grandparent's death

WHEN THEY SAY: *"I'm afraid I am going to forget Grandma."*

DON'T SAY: *"Of course you won't. I can't imagine why you would say that."*

SAY: *"I don't think you will, but our minds do forget details over time. Maybe you should create something to remember the details that are important to you. You could journal about times with Grandma or create a memory box or put together a photo album with captions. I am happy to help."*

BECAUSE: Stimulating the teen to keep memories alive rather than blocking them out helps affirm the value of the relationship. Doing "memory work" helps alleviate the worry she has that she will "lose" her grandmother.

MEMORY WORK TECHNIQUES

- Talk about memories and tell stories often of the person who died.
- Share keepsakes.
- Involve children in the funeral or other rituals.
- Display photos of the person who died.
- Visit special places that stimulate memories.
- Bring up the person who died whenever desired.
- Look over photo albums, family videos, or remember special times like holidays.
- Sing the favorite songs of the person who died.

WHEN THEY SAY: *"Grandma was my biggest fan. I feel lost without her."*

DON'T SAY: *"What do you mean? You have me, and I'm your fan, too."*

SAY: *"I know you and Grandma had a special bond and that makes it harder to live without her. You can still believe all the things she taught you about yourself. They are still true, even if she isn't here to remind you of them. How about you write them down and post them where you will see them every day?"*

BECAUSE: Oftentimes, a grandparent's love is uncomplicated. Because they don't have to discipline or take on the full responsibility of forming and shaping a child like a parent does, grandparents get to relax and simply play cheerleader and friend to their teenage grandchildren. If the two have a close relationship, the teen might be questioning her new self-identity now that Grandma is not around to reinforce her strengths and good qualities.

WHEN THEY SAY: *"What happens after we die?"*

DON'T SAY: *"Here's how it is..."*

SAY: *"I don't know, but this is what I personally think happens.... Everyone has to decide what's true for them."*

BECAUSE: The teen is starting to form philosophical beliefs about living, dying, and spirituality. What happens when we die is one of the greatest mysteries of life. It's OK to share your ideas about it, but empower him to explore this question for himself. It's also just fine to say, "I don't know, but we can explore it." Adults sometimes think they have to have all the answers. When we admit we don't really know, we help enhance his search for meaning.

WHEN THEY SAY: *"I miss Grandma so much; I feel like my heart has been ripped open."*

DON'T SAY: *"If it hurts too much, stay busy: Watch television, go to the movies, or get lost in a book."*

SAY: *"That is such a hard feeling. I feel it sometimes too. I wish I could take your pain away, but just know that feeling it is a part of your healing, and as time passes, it won't hurt as much."*

BECAUSE: In order to reconcile grief, we must pass through suffering. It's hard to see kids hurt, yet pain is part of the natural work of mourning. In part, we heal by embracing hurt. If we go through our grief rather than around it, we integrate the death of our loved one and eventually we are able to release the pain, accept the death, and go on to live and love fully, without hesitation. Unresolved grief doesn't dissipate with time. It needs the help of active mourning to be released.

WHAT IT MEANS TO DIE OF NATURAL CAUSES OR "OLD AGE"

When people die of "old age," they have died from natural, or biological, causes. Natural causes of death occur when the body stops working, like when arteries become clogged and oxygen is not carried to the heart and the heart stops pumping blood, or when someone gets sick from a disease, like cancer, or an illness, like meningitis, that attack the body from the inside. If the cause is a normal deterioration of the body, it's called natural.

Old age is not a true cause of death, in and of itself. It does, however, reflect a "natural" death versus an "unnatural" death. Unnatural death occurs when outside circumstances cause death, such as car accidents. Two-thirds of the deaths in the world are due to natural causes.

As we age, our bodies break down on the molecular and cellular level. Obvious external signs of aging are wrinkles and gray hair—which are the result of cells getting "old" and becoming less able to replicate themselves perfectly. As new cells form they are imperfect, contributing to the overall deterioration of the body.

To describe dying of old age to a child, consider saying: "As we grow older and older, our body parts are less and less able to do their jobs and keep the body running well, as they do when people are young. Imagine a brand new car. Now imagine an old clunker. In some ways, it's like that with people, but people can "age gracefully" by taking good care of their bodies—eating healthy foods, sleeping well, and getting plenty of exercise. Even so, every body eventually wears out. We all grow old and die."

"Until one has loved an animal,
a part of one's soul remains unawakened."

— ANATOLE FRANCE

CHAPTER SIX

When a pet dies

While a pet's death may seem trivial next to a family member's death, it's important to remember that to a child a pet may be seen as an equal member of the family (and to many of us adults as well). Pets provide unconditional, uncomplicated love and conjure up mostly good feelings for a child. When pets die, their comfort and unabashed joy are truly missed and mourned.

PRESCHOOLERS—AGES 3 TO 5
Talking to preschoolers about a pet's death

WHEN THEY SAY:	*"Luna was my best friend."*
DON'T SAY:	*"You are funny. A dog can't be your best friend."*
SAY:	*"It must feel really hard to have your best friend die. Can you tell me about it?"*
BECAUSE:	It's important not to discount your child's feelings of grief. He needs to know that you take his feelings seriously.

WHEN THEY SAY: *"I wish Sara would have died instead of Luna!"*

DON'T SAY: *"Shame on you! Of course you love your sister more than a dog!"*

SAY: *"I know you loved Luna very much and you miss her. Are you mad at your sister right now about something?"*

BECAUSE: Preschoolers live in the moment. The fact that her sister is being mean to her in the moment reminds her that she can't go snuggle her dog anymore for comfort. In that moment, she loves Luna more than she does her sister.

WHEN THEY SAY: *"Can we stuff Luna so I can keep her in my room?"*

DON'T SAY: *"That would be weird, don't you think?"*

SAY: *"No, but we can bury Luna (or Luna's ashes) in the yard, and we can make a sign that says, "Here lies Luna. She was a good dog."*

BECAUSE: The preschooler is simply stating a wish to be near his dog's body, or to preserve the dog and keep it around forever. Letting him be involved with how to dispose of the body is important to his healing. By participating he can better integrate that the death is real.

WHEN THEY SAY: *"I miss Luna!"*

DON'T SAY: *"Let's go to the pet shop and pick out a new dog."*

SAY: *"I know, sweetie. I miss Luna too. Do you remember the day we got Luna and how she (cried all the way home but stopped when you put her in your lap)?"*

BECAUSE: Replacing a pet too quickly cuts off a child's opportunity to mourn. Wait a while before getting another pet. If you act too soon, the child might feel guilty, thinking that she is being "unfaithful" to Luna. She might even reject the new puppy or try to hurt it. After some time passes, suggest finding another pet, explaining that it will never take the place of the previous pet.

SCHOOL-AGERS—AGES 6 TO 11
Talking to school-aged children about a pet's death

WHEN THEY SAY: *"Why did Luna have to die?"*

DON'T SAY: *"Luna was just a dog. We can always get another dog."*

SAY: *"Luna was a special part of our family. We will all miss her very much, but every living thing dies. She didn't do anything to deserve dying. It just happened."*

BECAUSE: To children, the death of a pet is serious business, especially when the death was unexpected and gruesome, like if Luna ran out and got hit by a car. Treat it as such and be patient with his questions.

WHEN THEY SAY: *"Do you think I killed Luna by (overfeeding her or letting her loose or not being nice)?"*

DON'T SAY: *"She sure was a fat dog."*

SAY: *"No. The veterinarian said that Luna died because her heart didn't work right and stopped beating. Remember? It wasn't your fault that Luna died."*

BECAUSE: Some children harbor guilt about not taking care of their pet, thinking they were "bad" owners and therefore they are responsible for the pet's death. Reassure her that she took good care of the dog and loved her very much—and that you also made sure the dog always had enough to eat and drink and a comfortable place to sleep.

WHEN THEY SAY: *"Did it hurt Luna when they put her down?"*

DON'T SAY: *"No, it was like putting her to sleep."*

SAY: *"No, when Luna was euthanized she didn't feel pain and she died quickly, ending her suffering."*

BECAUSE: The child needs to know that sleep and death are not the same thing. Also, reassure him that by euthanizing the pet, you really did her a favor because she was in a lot of pain. You can remind the child of the way the dog would whine or limp or show other outward signs of pain to ease any guilt he might be harboring.

WHEN THEY SAY: *"I'm the only one in this family that misses Luna!"*

DON'T SAY: *"Luna belonged to all of us, not just you."*

SAY: *"Is that how you feel? Maybe I haven't told you, or showed you enough, how much I miss Luna. I really do. She was such a great dog. I loved the way she.... What do you miss about her?"*

BECAUSE: The child, for whatever reason, is feeling alone in her grief for her pet. She is trying to provoke an opportunity to express her grief. Don't cut her off because she is angry. See her anger as hurt and pain and respond to it with love.

TEENAGERS—AGES 12 TO 19
Talking to teenagers about a pet's death

WHEN THEY SAY: *"I wish I would have spent more time with Luna."*

DON'T SAY: *"It's true. You are gone a lot, and you used to play with her more."*

SAY: *"It's normal for teenagers to spend more time with their friends than their families, and that means the family dog too. Don't feel bad about that. You had many good years of fun and love with Luna."*

BECAUSE: Teenagers often have mixed feelings when breaking away from their families during adolescence. Spending more time out in the world is not only appropriate but healthy. Reassure him that it was natural for him to have spent less time with the dog as he grew older. On the other hand, to a teen who is distancing himself from the family, he may have felt more bonded with the pet than the people. Validate his need to mourn this loss.

WHEN THEY SAY: *"I never want another dog."*

DON'T SAY: *"Of course you will."*

SAY: *"It's hard to imagine another dog in our lives, isn't it?"*

BECAUSE: Teenagers often have a strong sense of honor and loyalty—something they are learning about in their circle of friends. If you have ever voiced doubt about one of your teen's friends, you probably know this firsthand! This sense of "loyalty for her peeps" can extend to the dog, with whom she may have literally grown up and shared a special bond. Possibly, she felt the dog was there when no one else was, offering comfort in a time of need.

WHEN THEY SAY:	*"I don't want to forget Luna."*
DON'T SAY:	*"There will be other dogs in your life."*
SAY:	*"Why don't you journal about Luna and write down stories of her life? Or create a photo book about her?"*
BECAUSE:	Tapping into emotions isn't always easy for teenagers, especially when they've received the message that they should be "mature," which means "strong" and "stoic." Encouraging creative outlets for feelings lets him off the hook a bit and gives him a comfortable way to express his feelings. He may think it is silly or babyish to cry over a dog. Having a purpose or path for his grief helps.

WHEN THEY SAY:	*"Whatever, she was just a dog."*
DON'T SAY:	*"Shame on you! She was a good dog to you!"*
SAY:	*"She was much more than 'just a dog' to us, don't you think? She was really a part of the family. I really loved her, and I miss her. The house feels empty without her."*
BECAUSE:	Again, the need to be autonomous is sometimes expressed with the simple phrase "whatever" or "I don't care" by teens. They say what they think they should feel. Most likely, the teen feels something quite different if she lets herself. If you open up about your grief over the loss of the dog, she will see that it's something OK for "adults like her" to do. Whether or not she shows you is a different story and depends on the teen.

"There's no tragedy in life like the death of a child.
Things never get back to the way they were."

— DWIGHT D. EISENHOWER

CHAPTER SEVEN

When a friend or classmate dies

Children are not supposed to die. When they do, it's a shock for everyone involved. The reality is that sometimes children do die. When a classmate or friend dies, a child is profoundly impacted. Children feel most in tune and connected with children their own age. There is a strong sense of "we are in this together" and "what happens to you often happens to me." If she was close to the classmate who died, the child will feel a deep sense of loss. If she was not close, she will be curious and wonder why—and possibly take on fears of dying in the same way. Some children who experience the loss of a peer feel as if the foundation of their world is altered. Where they once felt safe, they no longer do. Usually, schools will offer grief support to students, but it's important to provide extra support at home and to watch for signs that a child might need extra help addressing her grief.

PRESCHOOLERS—AGES 3 TO 5
Talking to preschoolers about a classmate's or friend's death

WHEN THEY SAY: *"I made Madison die because I was mean to her."*

DON'T SAY: *"That's ridiculous. Don't think like that."*

SAY: *"Do you remember fighting with Madison? Words can make us feel sad or mad, but they can't kill us. You didn't kill Madison, honey. She died because her body broke, which hardly ever happens to kids."*
OR/AND:
"Friends fight sometimes. All friends do that. You also had some fun together, didn't you?"

BECAUSE: The child is feeling guilty about past times when she and the child who died didn't get along. Due to normal egocentrism, preschoolers can think that they control things that happen in their lives. Reassure her in a loving way that her friend's death had nothing to do with her.

WHEN THEY SAY: *"What does death mean?"*

DON'T SAY: *"I'll explain it to you when you are older."*

SAY: *"Do you know how when you smack a bug it stops moving? It is no longer alive, and it can't come back to life either. Death is the end of life, and all living things die. I know it is hard to understand."*

BECAUSE: While preschoolers might not completely understand death or that death is forever, it is good to answer their questions about death as best you can, and as often as they ask it. Come up with different examples and different ways to describe death. It may be something they ask over and over again in an attempt to understand.

WHEN THEY SAY: *"Can I go visit Madison in heaven?"*

DON'T SAY: *"No, because I don't want you to die!"*

SAY: *"Sorry, honey. You can't. Heaven is only for souls. Because you still live in your body you have to stay here on earth."*
OR:
"No, honey. Once someone dies they are gone and we can't see them again."

BECAUSE: The preschooler needs to know that when we die, we are gone for good and we can never come back. This realization is sad, but it helps her to begin her grieving process for her friend.

WHEN THEY SAY: *"My stomach hurts!"*

DON'T SAY: *"Oh, you must have caught a bug. Let's get you some medicine."*

SAY: *"You have been through a lot with Madison dying. Your body is saying that it is sad and it needs rest, love, and hugs right now. Let's get you some. In a while you will feel better."*

BECAUSE: At times of acute grief, a child's body responds to what the mind has been told. I've witnessed children in grief experiencing stomach pain, headaches, rashes, poor or extreme appetites, difficulty sleeping, tiredness, and shortness of breath. Help the child recognize these physical pains as normal and temporary. This will lessen his concern. Also, take these physical complaints as a cue that he is asking for extra care right now. Finally, it's not unusual for a young child to take on the pain of the person who died. For example, if his friend had nausea from chemotherapy, he might feel nauseated too.

SCHOOL-AGERS: AGES 6 TO 11
Talking to school-aged children about a classmate's or
friend's death

WHEN THEY SAY: *"I got in a fight at school today."*

DON'T SAY: *"Go to your room and think about what you did."*

SAY: *"People are supposed to live long, happy lives, but
once in a while a young person dies. This feels
unfair and can make us angry. When we get angry
and scared, we get agitated and confrontations can
happen. Do you think this happened to you today?
Have you been upset about Madison's death?"*

BECAUSE: It helps to think of "dark" emotions—anger, rage,
frustration, etc.—as outward protests to inward
feelings of hurt, fear, sadness, and worry. The
child is protesting his friend's death. He is also
expressing his confusion and fear in what feels
like a powerful way: through anger and action.
Remember, fear and anger are close cousins. Rather
than punishing the anger, try to get to the root of
the fear and help the child voice what he feels so
you can talk it through and come to some sort of
reconciliation. In my experience, grieving children
act out for four reasons: feelings of insecurity
(the landscape of his world has changed and
shifted), feelings of abandonment (feeling as if his
friend left him), a desire to provoke punishment
(an irrational belief that he is bad so therefore
he deserves punishment), and for protection
from future losses (if he pushes others away and
detaches from them, they can't hurt him by dying).

WHEN THEY SAY: *"How can I stop feeling sad?"*

DON'T SAY: *"Every time you think of Madison, stop yourself. Turn on some music or call another friend."*

SAY: *"It's natural to feel sad when someone you care about dies. That's a part of something called grief—the mix of emotions we feel after a death. At first it can hurt a lot. But if you are sad, don't pretend that you are not. That doesn't help. Sometimes it helps to do something, like write a letter to Madison's parents telling them what you liked about her and what you miss or hanging a picture of you two together in your room. If you feel your grief feelings, over time they start to hurt less and less."*

BECAUSE: Feeling deep sadness is painful, and we naturally resist pain. Help the child take her grief in "doses." Combine active mourning—like crying, talking about her friend, or making a memory item—with breaks from mourning. Often after a hard cry, we feel a little better or maybe even numb. It's natural to seek a balance between intense emotions and feeling numb, distracted, and at peace.

WHEN THEY SAY: *"Where did Madison go?"*

DON'T SAY: *"She lives in a big mansion in the sky."*

SAY: *"I believe there are three parts to people: a body, a mind, and a soul. The body is like a suit we wear, and when we die it breaks and can never be fixed. We usually put the body and mind, or brain, in the ground. The third part to people is the soul. The soul is the part of us that feels feelings like happiness and joy. I think this part lives on after someone dies. I think Madison's soul is in heaven. People think different things about where we go after we die,* *and no one knows for sure. But that's what I think. What do you think?"*

BECAUSE: The child is asking one of the great questions of life. It's hard to answer, and this is just one suggestion. Depending on the child's age and level of curiosity/maturity, you could explore your religion/beliefs or different religions and spiritual movements throughout the world.

WHEN THEY SAY: *"I'll never find a friend like Madison ever again!"*

DON'T SAY: *"You have plenty of friends."*

SAY: *"I know Madison was special to you. I understand why you miss her, and why you feel so sad that she died. What do you miss most about not having her around?"*

BECAUSE: The child is expressing her sadness over her friend's death. She is also letting you know that it left her feeling alone socially. Encourage her to express her grief feelings about her friend. Also, try to determine exactly what she is missing—maybe Madison was the only friend who still played Barbie dolls with her. Gently suggest other friends who might step into that role, always acknowledging that Madison can't be replaced, but that the child doesn't have to lose the activities she did with Madison, or the places they went.

WHEN THEY SAY: *"I don't want to go back to school."*

DON'T SAY: *"You have to. It's not an option. Now get ready this instant."*

SAY: *"I understand how it's hard to go back to school. After all, you and Madison were in the same class, and*

I know you played together a lot at recess. How about I call your teacher and let her know this is hard for you? I know she can't change it, but she can help you feel better about school."

BECAUSE: The child isn't rejecting school—he's rejecting being at school and feeling sad about his friend and missing her in public. Maybe he is afraid he will cry. Maybe he simply needs a break from mourning and it's too hard to imagine facing those feelings again. Take the time to provide comfort, even if it means you are late to school or work. Let him know you are available if he needs to be picked up during the day. If he simply can't go, don't force it; grieving must take precedence if he is to heal. Let the school staff know that your child is struggling. Schools often have resources set up to help children cope after the death of a classmate. The counselor may even hold assemblies or counseling sessions in classrooms to help kids process their grief as a group. Children feel support from others during the process.

WHEN DEATH IS SUDDEN AND TRAUMATIC

No matter the form, death is hard when someone we love dies. Yet when it's sudden and traumatic—as with a car accident, workplace accident, murder, or suicide—it's especially so. Children who survive such tragedies need extra compassion and care. I've found the following to be common characteristics of grief when sudden, traumatic deaths happen.

- **Complicated grief.**
  Traumatic, sudden death complicates grief. Everything is intensified, including shock, confusion, disorganization, fear, vulnerability, guilt, and anger. The death will feel extra unfair.

- **Intense anger.**
  Sudden deaths, especially violent ones, may bring up feelings of intense anger and a sense of injustice. They might even create a desire for revenge. The child might burst into a rage. Try to remember that anger is not wrong or bad and resist trying to tame the anger. When expressed fully, it begins to lose some of its power. Should the child begin to act out the anger in destructive ways, part of your helping role is to set appropriate boundaries.

- **Feeling unsafe.**
  With sudden deaths, a child feels extra vulnerable and threatened. The quick shift from feeling safe to realizing such things happen is shocking. Fears may surface about his safety and his own mortality. He may experience anxiety and panic attacks.

- **Why, why, and why?**
  The question of "why" comes up often. The child struggles with understanding how something like this can happen. Don't feel a need to answer the "why." Simply create a space of acceptance and openness that allows her to think out loud, talk, scream, play, and wail without judgment or limits (as long as safety is guarded).

- **A need for counseling.**
  With sudden, traumatic deaths, consider professional grief counseling to supplement your companion role.

TEENAGERS—AGES 12 TO 19
Talking to teenagers about a classmate's or friend's death

WHEN THEY SAY: *"I can't believe this happened."*

DON'T SAY: *"Bad things happen every day. It's too bad it had to happen to Maddie."*

SAY: *"It might take a while to sink in, and that's OK. You are in shock right now, and that's normal when you find out someone has died. Shock means you feel disbelief and numbness. You may be unable to believe it happened, or you may want to deny that Maddie died. Is that how you feel? Try to be patient and gentle with yourself. What would make you feel better right now?"*

BECAUSE: The teen might be in shock, especially if the death was sudden. Shock represents a variety of emotions, such as disbelief, numbness, and denial, as well as physiological symptoms. She might seem numb and go through her days on automatic pilot. Some teens say they can't cry. Shock is one of the first responses to death. The teen might feel surprised by the realization that "Maddie's dead" over and over again, feeling disbelief each time that she realizes it. Don't react to the apparent lack of feelings. It's just that children sometimes need to take in the reality of the death in little snippets or "doses" because it's too big to comprehend all at once.

WHEN THEY SAY: *"What's wrong with me? I can't think straight!"*

DON'T SAY: *"Try to push thoughts of Maddie out of your head and focus on what you are doing."*

SAY: *"That must feel scary, but please know that it's a*

*natural response when someone you care about dies.
It's a normal part of grief to feel confused and not
think straight."*

OR/AND:

*"You are not losing your mind! This forgetfulness
and distractedness will go away when things settle
down. Your memory will return to normal. For now,
take it easy and don't schedule too much."*

BECAUSE: A common response the first few weeks or months
after a death is disorganization and panic. Teens
might forget assignments, miss practices, lock
keys in cars, forget their lunch, and feel generally
discombobulated. That's because so many thoughts
are running through their heads as they try to
"figure out" the death. He might be thinking, "Will
I die like that too?" or "Who will I eat lunch with
now?" or "Life is not fair," and so on. Encourage
crying and talking to take its natural course. Let
him talk, even when it doesn't make sense. Be
patient and remember that you are a caregiver, not
a curegiver.

WHEN THEY SAY: *"I can't stop picturing how Maddie died."*

DON'T SAY: *"Maybe I better get you in to a counselor."*

SAY: *"When something shocking and traumatic happens,
it gets stuck in our brains, and we keep replaying it,
hoping to figure it out. That's really normal. I know
it's disturbing to have a flashback in the middle of
math class or wake up from a nightmare about
Maddie's death. Try not to be alarmed. It helps to tell
someone about it or even to write about it. Over
time, it will happen less and less."*

BECAUSE: Having flashbacks or dreams is simply our

subconscious brain trying to process shocking and confusing information. It's normal to dream about the person who died, especially when it was sudden and traumatic. If this persists, it would be very appropriate to seek consultation from a trained grief counselor who works with grieving teens.

WHEN THEY SAY: *"We just have to accept Maddie's death. I mean, bad things happen, right?"*

DON'T SAY: *"You are right. That's a good attitude. There's nothing we can do about it anyway, so we might as well not think about it."*

SAY: *"It's true that Maddie died and you can't change it. Just know that if you start feeling sad about it, or want to cry about it, I hope you do. There is no right or wrong way to deal with this, so whatever you feel is OK. I'm always here if you ever need to talk."*

BECAUSE: Sometimes, teens in grief think they need to act hypermature and "grown up" about a death. The danger of sustained hypermaturity in the face of death is displaced grief—grief that is stifled and not allowed to surface and therefore spreads out in the mind, body, and soul, causing undesired symptoms. The teen might become increasingly anxious and agitated. Or he might seem overly tired and drained. He might become depressed and detach from people and activities that usually bring him meaning. Explore with the teen where this attitude came from. Are his peers or adults in his life giving him the message to "be strong" or "handle this like a man?" Truthfully, we can't put things behind us before we are ready. To truly "move on" and reconcile grief, we must allow grief in and then let it out.

WHEN THEY SAY: *"I don't care about anything. Just go away."*

DON'T SAY: *"OK, you need your space, I get it."*

SAY: *"It's normal when someone you care about dies to feel deeply sad and even depressed. I get that. But you need to talk with someone about how you feel, whether it's me, your friends, Aunt Jean, or a counselor. I know it seems easier to just ignore it, but in the long run it just makes it harder. Who seems like the best person to talk with about Maddie's death and how it makes you feel?"*

BECAUSE: When the full sense of loss sets in, teens can feel sad, empty, and depressed. Depression is a normal reaction to a significant loss or death. A depressed teen might show little interest in herself or others, withdraw, be unable to experience joy or pleasure, feel low about herself, and eat and drink poorly. It's important to keep a close eye on her and encourage her to connect with others as continued depression can lead to complicated mourning.

"Suicide is death by just another name, but the implications and stigma that surround its mystery and aftermath are strong enough to touch every facet of our lives and of society."

— NAN & GARY ZASTROW

CHAPTER EIGHT

When someone dies by suicide

Because of the social stigma around suicide, survivors often suffer in silence, complicating the healing that comes from active, open mourning. With suicide there is the general belief that it is wrong and that it shouldn't be discussed. Children who are close to someone who dies by suicide especially feel abandoned and alone during a time when they desperately need unconditional support and understanding. They've been hit with a triple whammy—not only have they experienced a death, they've experienced a sudden, traumatic death—and on top of that a stigmatized one. Survivors of suicide often feel intense or explosive emotions and feelings of guilt, fear, and shame, along with a feeling of "if only." These feelings of anguish and remorse may be expressed as temper tantrums, physical risk taking, and with teens, alcohol and drug use to "bury" the pain. As a companion, you must listen with your heart and break down the silence that engulfs this difficult death.

PRESCHOOLERS—AGES 3 TO 5
Talking to preschoolers about suicide

WHEN THEY SAY: *"How did Uncle Matthew die?"*

DON'T SAY: *"You are too young to understand. I will tell you when you are older."*
OR:
"We don't want to talk about that."

SAY: *"Do you know how our bodies can get sick? Well, Uncle Matthew's brain got sick and it hurt so bad that he chose to stop living."*

BECAUSE: When talking about suicide or a stigmatized death with a preschooler, you need to be honest, but you don't want to go into great detail. Start simple and see if a brief explanation satisfies. If she asks more questions, answer each with a subsequent short answer. Don't lie. If her questions lead to a discussion of how Uncle Matthew died by suicide (with pills, a gun, a rope, etc.), be honest, but always let her questions guide the conversation.

WHEN THEY SAY: *"Was he mad at me? Is that why he went away?"*

DON'T SAY: *"I don't think so, honey. No one knows for sure why he died."*

SAY: *"Uncle Matthew loved you very much. You were one of his favorite people in the world. You didn't do anything to make him die."*

BECAUSE: Preschoolers believe they are at the center of the world. The danger of this developmental stage is that preschoolers can assume they caused something to happen. Reassure him that he had nothing to do with the death.

WHEN THEY SAY: *"What happened to Uncle Matthew?"*

DON'T SAY: *"Uncle Matthew got cancer and died."*

SAY: *"Uncle Matthew died by suicide. Suicide means that he ended his own life. He's dead and he can't ever come alive again. I know it is confusing and sad. Will you come sit on my lap so I can give you a hug?"*

BECAUSE: The very youngest children may not be ready or able to comprehend the news of a suicide, but older preschool children often benefit from the truth. Someday they will find out about the suicide— whether now, when the police come to visit, or later, from siblings or cousins. They may feel betrayed by your dishonesty. Parents who chose to hide the suicide from their children tell me that they always feel pressure and stress around keeping the secret and that they live in fear of blurting it out. It's often a relief when they are able to tell the child the truth about the death.

WHEN THEY SAY: *"Go away!"*

DON'T SAY: *"OK, goodbye!"*

SAY: *"You seem really mad right now. Are you mad? Are you mad that Uncle Matthew died? It's OK if you want some quiet time alone for a bit, but come see me soon, OK?"*

BECAUSE: Preschoolers might be frustrated about not being able to express how they feel about the death. It takes a lot of words, some they don't know yet, to talk about all the intense feelings they have inside. Anger can be a catch-all for the confusion, pain, insecurity, and fear the child feels inside, as well as what he senses from others. He may also simply be angry that no one is paying him the attention he needs. Help him get his feelings out through physical movement—chasing, dancing, or playing a game will help him release the pressure he feels inside. Art—drawing, painting, creating clay figures, etc.—is another way for him to "talk" about his grief. Finally, don't be alarmed if the death becomes a common theme in his make-believe play. It may strike you as cruel or crude, but it's just his way of processing this complicated death.

SCHOOL-AGERS: AGES 6 TO 11
Talking to school-aged children about suicide

WHEN THEY SAY: *"What is suicide?"*

DON'T SAY: *"Oh, you never mind that."*

SAY: *"Suicide happens when someone gets very depressed, which is like being sad times 100 without a break. It hurts a lot, and it makes a person want to stop the hurt, and the only way he thinks he can is to stop living."*

BECAUSE: There's a good chance that word of the suicide will get around, and if you don't talk with the child about it, he may hear about it at school or at the funeral or at the next family get-together. Worse yet, he may get the message that he shouldn't talk about the death. He needs to hear about the suicide from you first. That way you can do your best to welcome questions and openly accept his intense feelings. Hiding just causes shame—something he doesn't need on top of all he is sorting through right now. And if he asks questions about how the person died by suicide? Answer them, straightforwardly and honestly.

WHEN THEY SAY: *"It doesn't make sense. He seemed fine the last time we saw him."*

DON'T SAY: *"Well, I guess we should have checked in with him more."*

SAY: *"It's true. He was laughing and was even playing football with you guys. Even though he looked happy on the outside, he was experiencing something difficult on the inside. We couldn't help because we didn't know."*

BECAUSE: Suicide causes a lot of confusion. Your child naturally wants to figure it out. Allow him to do it in his own way. He may need to chew on it a while and try to understand it through thinking, talking, and playing.

WHEN THEY SAY: *"I just wish everyone would stop talking about it!"*

DON'T SAY: *"How can we stop when it is all we can think of? We have to talk about it."*

SAY: *"It sounds like we need a break from talking about Matthew's suicide. Let's plan a little get-away and go camping this weekend and focus on having fun."*

BECAUSE: She is expressing that she is overwhelmed with the suicide and needs a mental and emotional break from it. Children grieve in "doses" and can only let in so much pain at a time. Honor this desire to step out of it for a while. Show her the other side of life—that joy and fun still exist. She also might be overwhelmed by the details of what happened, feeling like she isn't old enough to handle them. The next time it's being discussed, ask her if she wants to stay and hear or leave the room. Also, planning time in nature provides a space of calmness and helps reset us when we are overwhelmed.

WHEN THEY SAY: *"I miss him so much."*

DON'T SAY: *"I know, but you need to let him go."*
OR:
"What's done is done. We can't change it so we better just move on."

SAY: *"I know what you are feeling. I miss him too. Sometimes, I miss him so much I feel like I might* *explode. Do you ever feel that way?"*

BECAUSE: The child's grief cannot be rushed. He will need many opportunities to feel, and express, his grief. While it may seem like remembering him will only cause pain, don't forget that pain is healing. He can't go around grief, he must go through it. Give him many chances to express his grief through words, crying, actions, ceremony, and play.

TEENAGERS—AGES 12 TO 19
Talking to teenagers about suicide

WHEN THEY SAY: *"Why did he do it?"*

DON'T SAY: *"He just gave up on life."*

SAY: *"We may never know why. If you can, accept the not knowing. It is a mystery, and mysteries are for pondering, not solving."*
OR/AND:
"I don't know for sure, but I do know he was very tortured by life and just didn't know how to stop his pain, or what he was trying didn't work. I know it's hard to understand. I struggle with it too. I do know he really cared for you, though, and his death had nothing to do with you."

BECAUSE: "Why" is the most common question asked after a suicide. Naturally, we want things to make sense, and suicide is often deeply personal. When we are confronted with suicide, we face a mystery. Encourage the teen to accept that she may never have the answer to why; encourage the teen to accept the mystery and instead embrace and open to the idea of eventual healing. Grieving teens need our help if they are to survive what to them often seems unsurvivable.

WHEN THEY SAY: *"How could she do that to us?! I'm so mad at her!"*

DON'T SAY: *"Are you sure you were a good friend to her?"*

SAY: *"When Maggie decided to end her life, I doubt she was thinking of you, her other friends, her family, or anyone for that matter. If she was, she probably wasn't thinking straight and thought you'd all be better off without her or something senseless like*

*that. Her death wasn't about you or anyone else. It
was about herself."*

BECAUSE: Usually when people kill themselves, they are
doing it out of self-anguish, not to hurt somebody
else. In fact, suicidal people often make statements
along the lines of: "If I am gone it will be easier for
them." The grieving teen may vacillate between
sadness, hurt, and outright anger. She may feel
betrayed and left behind. Let her know that her
anger is normal and necessary, and help her find
healthy ways to express it. It's also important for
her to find a way to say goodbye. She can write
her friend a letter, for example, or have a private
ceremony with her group of friends or classmates.

WHEN THEY SAY: *"The world is a terrible place. No wonder he
wanted to leave it!"*

DON'T SAY: *"He just chickened out."*

SAY: *"Life can get overwhelming. There are hard things
we often have to face in life, but there is a lot of
good, even if it is difficult to see that all of the time.
Matthew may have been stuck in just seeing
challenges. The best way you can honor him is to
seek the joy and happiness he couldn't find. If you
feel stuck, who can you talk with about it? Have you
participated in the peer groups at school? How about
I take you to that teen support group that meets
on Wednesdays?"*

BECAUSE: Suicide, especially when a teen dies by suicide, can
have a chain-reaction effect among classmates.
Maybe you've heard the term "copycat suicide."
Teenagers are discovering life and often have
passionate "awakenings" about world happenings.

They might get impassioned about global warming, genocide, war, and other atrocities. After all, it's the age when they are exposed to challenging topics and start seeing the world for what it is—the good, the bad, and the ugly. When a friend or classmate dies by suicide, the teen might feel an intense loyalty. She might irrationally think that it's honorable to "stand beside" her friend and die by suicide herself. Listen closely for defeating comments or statements that her "friend was right." If you suspect she may be planning a suicide, waste no time in getting help.

WHEN THEY SAY: *"I can't breathe!" Or, "I think I'm having a heart attack!"*

DON'T SAY: *"Take it easy. You will be fine."*

SAY: *"You might be feeling what's called a panic attack. It's common when you feel shocked and scared after a suicide. I know it feels really scary, but it will pass and no damage will be done. Lie down and let me help you relax. We can visit with the doctor about other solutions."*

BECAUSE: Fear, panic, and withdrawal are common responses to sudden death and suicide. The teen might be worrying that someone else close to him will die by suicide, or he may be simply reacting to the shock and disbelief that come with suicide grief. His head is swimming, and he feels a prolonged and heightened sense of unreality and anxiety. Panic attacks are an intense feeling of pending danger, even when there is no real danger coming. Symptoms include shortness of breath, dizziness, feeling faint, labored breathing, and a racing heart. A heavy pain in the chest can also be felt, making it feel to the teen like he is having a heart attack. Consider seeing a professional counselor if the attacks become more frequent.

WHEN THEY SAY: *"To heck with it! I'm out of here. There's a party tonight and I am going."*

DON'T SAY: *"Go ahead; you deserve it."*

SAY: *"I know it's tempting to want to escape the pain. I get it. But drugs and alcohol are like band-aids. They make you feel better for a bit, but you end up feeling worse afterwards. Go have fun, but please be safe and make good choices. Check in when you get home, OK?"*

BECAUSE: The intense feelings sudden deaths like suicide create often feel like they need an intense reaction from the teen, whose grief is naturally complicated during this turbulent developmental stage. He may get caught up in a group protest of a friend's death. Or, he might be feeling outrage and injustice over the idea that such awful things happen in life. He might also party to protest or drown the realization that young people die—and that he could die too. Plus, he might want to "tempt" death out of loyalty for his friend. Finally, many teens drink or do drugs after a death to experience temporary relief from the deep pain they feel—something hard to resist when you live in the moment, as teens often do. Help him find healthy ways to express his pain, such as playing or listening to music, getting exercise, participating in sports, being in nature, writing, talking, or doing something positive in his friend's name (like taking over her volunteer duties or contacting her parents).

STIGMATIZED DEATHS: SUICIDE, AIDS, HOMICIDE

Sometimes there is a stigma surrounding the nature of the death; the greater the stigma, generally the less the support available to the child and family as they mourn. Examples of stigmatized deaths include those from AIDS, suicide, homicide, and drug overdose. My colleague Ken Doka has described losses that cannot be openly acknowledged, socially sanctioned, or publicly mourned as "disenfranchised grief" experiences. The potential of stigma should always be kept in mind as you companion a bereaved child. As she might be getting the social message that the death shouldn't be discussed, continually invite her to talk about it and to ask questions so she understands she can be open about her feelings despite the nature of the death.

"Nothing good ever comes of violence."

— MARTIN LUTHER

CHAPTER NINE

When someone dies by homicide or manslaughter

Today's children are exposed to violent deaths—they see them in movies, cartoons, video games, and on the news. Sometimes, sadly, they experience such a death in their own lives. When a child is personally impacted by a sudden, traumatic death at the hands of another—through homicide or manslaughter—she experiences overwhelming grief, complicated by a loss of faith in human goodness and a realization that people can be not just careless, but sometimes cruel. Death by homicide results in survivors grieving not only the death, but how the person died. The senseless act brings on overwhelming feelings of turmoil, distrust, injustice, and helplessness. Survivors of murder victims enter into a world that is not understood by most people.

Unfortunately, members of a community where a tragic murder has occurred sometimes blame the victim or survivors as a shield to protect themselves from the truth that such awful things can happen so close to home. Child survivors are often left feeling numb and shocked for weeks and even months, and may have a hard time acknowledging the reality of the death. They need your loving care and extra support from others immediately and ongoing for weeks and months following the death.

PRESCHOOLERS—AGES 3 TO 5

Talking to preschoolers about homicide and manslaughter

WHEN THEY SAY: *"How did Joshua die?"*

DON'T SAY: *"That's only for adults to talk about."*

SAY: *"Joshua got in a car accident. Another car crashed into his car. His car broke and he was killed."*
OR:
"Joshua was out at night walking in the city. A bad man tried to steal his wallet. They fought and the bad man killed him."

BECAUSE: Whether or not he catches wind of all the details, the preschooler will understand that something big and bad has happened. Most likely police will visit, media stories might run, and adults, older siblings, neighbors, and relatives will talk. It will be impossible to completely shelter him from the news, and the snippets he hears might be even more frightening. On the other hand, you don't want him to hear details he can't handle. Try to appease him with as short an explanation as possible. You might be surprised that he is satisfied with this. Telling him nothing, or that he's too young to know, will create a shroud of secrecy and shame around the incident. You want him to trust you and feel safe with you, so honesty is best.

WHEN THEY SAY: *"I'm scared the man will kill me like he killed Joshua."*

DON'T SAY: *"Don't worry. That won't happen."*

SAY: *"I would never let that happen. The police are*

watching out for us and look, we have extra locks on the windows and doors. I know it is awful how your cousin Joshua died, but that hardly ever happens to people. I really don't believe it will happen to you, but how about you sleep in my room tonight so you feel better?"

BECAUSE: The young child may have made the horrific realization that people kill other people—in real life, not just movies. Intense fear and helplessness are common early responses to tragedies. She needs concrete proof that she, and her family, will be protected. If police are involved, have a police officer reassure her that protection is available for the family. Show her how the house is securely locked and how the security system works, if one exists. Let her sleep with you or in a sleeping bag in your room for extra comfort. Also, reassure her that while the death was terrible and tragic, murders (or manslaughters) don't usually happen to people. She may not completely understand as her world is still so small, but say it anyway because she will carry that truth as she grows.

WHEN THEY SAY: *"I don't want to ride in the car. I don't want to die like Joshua!"*

DON'T SAY: *"You have no choice. We have to ride in the car to get places. Now get in."*

SAY: *"I know it's scary and sad that Joshua died in a car accident, but that doesn't mean you will. Lots of people ride in cars every day and are never hurt. How about we ride our bikes to the grocery store today instead of the car? But next time we will have to take the car."*

OR:

> *"I'm sorry, but we have to ride in the car today. I understand that you are scared, and I promise I will drive extra, extra safe. How about we have Aunt Jen sit in back with you and put her arm around you the whole way? And here is your Hugga Bear. He is big and strong. You can hold onto him while we drive."*

BECAUSE: If the child's cousin died in a car accident, he might develop a fear of cars. This is especially true if he was involved in the accident himself. Respect that his fear is very real. If you do decide to drive, he may cry and express anxiety the entire time because in his mind, another car is sure to hit you and he will die. It's a tricky situation. If possible, take a break from cars and let the intensity of the fear subside. Or, initially, take very short trips. Remember, his fear is enhanced by the shock and grief of his cousin's recent death. Allowing time to untangle the two may help. When you do need to ride in the car, create a lot of extra comfort and talk with him the entire time to assuage his fears. Explain that your car has special safety powers called airbags and antilock brakes, and that his car seat is made to keep him safe. Over time and with successful trips, his anxiety will subside.

WHEN THEY SAY: *"Don't leave me!"*

DON'T SAY: *"I have to go to work. Now be a big girl and help me out."*

SAY: *"Come here and snuggle with me and let's talk a bit. Did you know Miss Claire is waiting to see you? And all your friends will be there, too. Anna is probably waiting to play your special game with you. Only you know the rules so she needs you. How about I take you there and I stay for the first half hour. Then, when playtime starts, I will go to work. I will* *tell Miss Claire that if you need to talk with me she should dial my number and give you the phone. And here is my special charm for you to carry in your pocket. It's to remind you that I am thinking of you and that we will see each other again soon."*

BECAUSE: When someone dies, young children can regress to old behaviors. They are scared and confused, and they need comfort and reassurance. Being away from you is hard because you equal safety and security. Ease the situation by setting up extra support and ways for her to access you for reassurance. Most likely when she gets to preschool or daycare, she will get involved and forget the need to be with you.

FINDING THE WORDS WHEN SOMEONE GOES MISSING

Traumatic, senseless deaths often leave families feeling shattered and ripped apart. When the loved one hasn't died but rather goes missing, feelings are even more complicated. If it is a child whose fate is uncertain, parents are often struck with a sense of sheer terror and panic. They bounce back and forth between hope and despair depending on the progress of the case. In these situations, people often mark two dates of death—the day the person went missing and the day her body was found. The waiting becomes torture in itself. If you are a non-family member, let the family know that you are available 24/7, to talk with, walk with, vent with, or assist in any way you can. Offer to do the hard jobs, like contacting the police for more information or thanking volunteer search parties.

What words are best in such difficult situations? If you are companioning a child or a whole family, let your heart, not your head, guide you. Resist saying things to make them feel better, such as, "I am sure they will find her alive." Instead, say: "There are no words for what you must be experiencing." Remember, you can't take away their pain, but you can make them feel less alone. In the same vein, don't be afraid to talk about the person and name her by name. For example: "I saw a book the other day on frogs and I thought about how much Isabel loves frogs." Those left behind fear that other people will forget their child. If the missing is long-term or after the body is found and holidays roll around, let the family know you understand how intense their pain must be by saying, "I know it must feel impossible not to have Isabel here for Christmas." Then settle in and listen, or better yet, lean forward to share a hug and tears with them.

SCHOOL-AGERS—AGES 6 TO 11
Talking to school-aged children about homicide and manslaughter

---

WHEN THEY SAY: *"Tell me again about the night Joshua died."*

DON'T SAY: *"Please don't ask about that. I don't want to talk about it."*

SAY: *"OK. I'll tell you again about the accident. Is there something you are trying to figure out? Is that why you want to hear it again?"*

BECAUSE: When such tragedies happen, people can get stuck replaying the scene over and over in their heads. It's the mind's natural way of trying to make sense of the senseless. As best you can, indulge the child and encourage supportive friends and relatives to step in if it's too hard for you. This shock and obsession is a part of the grief process for the child, and it shouldn't be stifled. Each time the incident is talked about, it loses a little more of its punch. A constant replay of the incident that doesn't let up may be a sign of post-traumatic stress syndrome (PTSD)—especially if the child witnessed the death. While PTSD isn't uncommon in the first weeks, if it continues seek the help of a professional quickly. Signs that extra help is needed include the child becoming more and more agitated, confused, distressed, and obsessed with the death incident.

WHEN THEY SAY: *"This isn't real. This only happens in movies."*

DON'T SAY: *"Try not to think about it."*

SAY: *"You are in shock right now, so it is hard to believe this happened. It's a terrible tragedy, and it is awful that such things happen in life. I am extra sorry it happened to you. As time passes it won't feel so* *raw and so powerful. You may not feel much but disbelief right now, but if that changes, know that it is OK to cry. And know that I am always here for you no matter what time of day or night."*

BECAUSE: The shock that something so terrible could happen in his family is incomprehensible to the child. Homicide is one of the worst experiences a family can have. It's natural to want to deny that it happened at first, and the sheer shock of it makes it seem surreal. Shock is a generic term that subsumes a variety of emotions, such as disbelief, numbness, and denial, as well as physiological responses. Admonishments like, "Be strong," "You shouldn't cry," and "You have to carry on" often encourage the suppression of emotions and as a result reinforce a prolonged sense of denial. If after weeks have passed the child continues to voice a total denial of the death, seek extra help.

WHEN THEY SAY: *"Why did he kill Joshua? Joshua was a good person! Why couldn't it have been someone else?"*

DON'T SAY: *"Don't be irrational. You are not thinking straight."*

SAY: *"I know it makes no sense and you are right: it is unfair. You know, it can help to write about it. How about you write a letter to the bad person and tell him how awful it feels to be without Joshua, and we will send it to him in prison?"*

BECAUSE: Anger is a common response to homicide and manslaughter. The death is unfair and no one should have to die in such violent ways. It's normal for the child to feel mad at the person who caused the death (especially if they were at fault or the death was intentional). It's also normal to feel mad at the world, or even mad that someone else lived and the person the child loved died. Since he can't confront the killer in person, it can feel empowering to the child to do it in make-believe play, through storytelling, drawing, or in writing. Encourage lots of different outlets for expressing feelings.

WHEN THEY SAY: *"Did it hurt?"*

DON'T SAY: *"Definitely not."*

SAY: *"I don't know for sure, but maybe not. Often the first feeling we get when our bodies get hurt is numbness. So maybe he died before this feeling wore off and the pain kicked in. Let's hope that is true."*

BECAUSE: Knowing a loved one suffered is hard to hear. Usually, we don't honestly know the answer to this question, and it is OK to err on the side of hope that the person didn't die in pain.

TEENAGERS—AGES 12 TO 19
Talking to teenagers about homicide and manslaughter

WHEN THEY SAY: *"I am going to find that guy and kill him!"*

DON'T SAY: *"Don't talk that way! It hurts enough without that kind of talk."*

SAY: *"I hear your anger. I am really angry at him for driving drunk and killing her too."*

BECAUSE: Rage fantasies are common for teens, especially when "unfair" deaths like car accidents or homicides happen. Try not to be frightened by this rage. It's a normal grief response, and most teens know they won't act on these feelings. The young person's heightened emotions often take the form of rage after a sudden death. Anger is a way for the teen to say, "I protest this death" and to vent her feelings of helplessness. Mostly, they want to have their feelings validated and for other people to voice that yes, it was an atrocity. It was unjust.

WHEN THEY SAY: *"Joshua won't be here to see me graduate."*

DON'T SAY: *"That's not really what's important here, is it?"*

SAY: *"That must feel hard. I know graduation is an important time for you, and you want everyone you love to share it with you. I am sorry he can't be here, but the rest of us will be right beside you."*

BECAUSE: Teens often do "catch-up" mourning at developmental milestones. Important events like prom or high school graduation may cause the grieving teen to feel particularly sad because the person who died isn't there to share the moment. This occurrence is normal not only shortly after the death, but also years later. In fact, many grieving teens will continue to do catch-up mourning as they enter adulthood and reach other milestones, like marrying or having children.

WHEN THEY SAY: *"How could God let this happen?"*

DON'T SAY: *"It was God's will. We can't question it."*

SAY: *"Sometimes things can't be easily explained. I personally don't believe God had a plan to punish us or have Joshua die such a cruel death. But I don't understand why it happened, either. I do have hope that someday it won't hurt so much, though."*

BECAUSE: Since teens are starting to form their separate sense of spirituality, it's natural that they will question the religious beliefs of their parents—and when a tragic death happens this process will be expedited. He may express doubts about long-held beliefs. Be open to this challenge. If he isn't allowed to wrestle with doubt, his faith will have little meaning now and in the future.

WHEN THEY SAY: *"I can't wait to see that guy locked away forever!"*

DON'T SAY: *"We forbid you to go to the trial."*

SAY: *"I want you to think long and hard about whether or not you want to go to the trial. You might hear things you don't want to hear, and the gruesome details might stick with you for a long time. Also, I know you hurt and you want to see justice. I do, too, but please know that his conviction won't end our pain or the grief you feel."*

BECAUSE: Depending on the teen's age, parents must decide if she can handle the trial. An older teen might insist, and barring her from it could cause long-term resentment. Consider picking and choosing which days of the trial she will attend, and bring along noise-canceling headphones just in case she can't leave the trial but decides she doesn't want to hear what's happening. You can compromise that she can be there beforehand or after—or that she gets a debriefing of happenings from you at the end of a trial day. Or, let her write a letter to the jury about what the murderer took away and how hard it is to live without her loved one. It may never be read, but it will help her feel like she did something to support the person who died—and also give her a vehicle to express her pain.

COMPANIONING WHEN VIOLENT ATTACKS HAPPEN AT SCHOOL OR IN THE COMMUNITY

In Colorado, where I live and practice, we have had our share of violent acts carried out by disenfranchised people—first there were the Columbine High School shootings in 1999 and, more recently, the Aurora movie theatre massacre in 2012. When such tragedies happen, grief is naturally complicated. Children will feel intense feelings of anger, confusion, disorganization, fear, vulnerability, and guilt churning around inside of them and surfacing sometimes all at once, resulting in temper tantrums, wailing, sadness, disbelief, or a complete denial due to the enormity of it all. The tragedy violates everything they ever believed about the world and people.

Depending on a child's age, awareness of what happened may not sink in or be fully understood until she grows older, resulting in grief awakenings over time. When companioning children who have lost someone they love, keep an extra eye open for signs that they are stuck in complicated grief—chronic depression, hopelessness, hostility, denial, panic, or fear. Try your best to restore her faith in humankind. Expose her to the outpouring of love and concern from neighbors, friends, classmates, and the community at large. Encourage her to tell you, or show you, her unique pain and grief through talking, playing, games, art, music, and more. If the child is a part of the school where the attack happened, encourage (but do not force) her to attend group support events at the school. Help her find a way, when she is ready, to say goodbye to her classmates or friends. Now, more than ever, accept grief on grief's terms.

"When you arise in the morning, think of what a precious privilege it is to be alive—to breathe, to enjoy, to love."

— MARCUS AURELIUS

CHAPTER TEN

When someone close has a terminal or life-threatening illness

When children learn that a family member is seriously ill, they usually feel shock and numbness at first. There might be thoughts like: "This can't be happening to us!", along with a belief that such hardships only happen to other people or in movies or the nightly news. Children will first understand it in their heads—and may ask a lot of questions about it—but it will take weeks or months to understand it in their hearts. They can only cope with the new reality this brings in doses. It will be tempting to promise that "Dad will get better," but it's healthier to be honest about the situation. You can still express hope, of course, but without false promises. Be patient with the unfolding of the child's grief. While he might understand it is a serious situation, he may not grasp that it could end in death. His grief will reflect his understanding and awareness of the situation, which will not be apparent all at once.

PRESCHOOLERS—AGES 3 TO 5
Talking to preschoolers about a terminal or life-threatening illness

---

WHEN THEY SAY: *"Why can't the doctors fix Daddy?"*

DON'T SAY: *"Doctors are smart. I bet they will be able to figure this out."*

SAY: *"Doctors don't have magical powers to fix people. They are doing their best, but sometimes people's bodies break and they can't be fixed."*

BECAUSE: Remember how the preschooler's mind has just a thin veil between real and imaginary? It's important that she stay in reality and not have high or false expectations, especially when the outlook is not good. Boil down medical explanations to their simplest form, and answer questions the child has about medical happenings as well as you can. She needs to feel included, which will help ease fears and feelings of abandonment.

WHEN THEY SAY: *"No! I just want to stay here with Daddy!"*

DON'T SAY: *"Come, now. You must go to preschool. Be good and help out."*

SAY: *"How about this. What if I have Ms. Anne, the neighbor, come over for a little while and watch you so you have extra time with Daddy today? Then, after a bit, she will take you to preschool. That way you get to spend extra time with him and still get to see your friends at preschool!"*

BECAUSE: The child is expressing his need to be near Dad. He might feel an overall heightened sense of anxiety and insecurity, and being with Dad makes him feel safer and more in control. After all, Dad can't die when he is there with him, right? Yet it is important to maintain his routine as much as possible. Enlist the help of friends and family, who truly want to help—more than you know. Most likely they simply need to be told what to do. Ask a friend or trusted adult to spend time with the child each day; he needs extra attention right now, when everyone is giving attention to the person who is sick, so having a dedicated person involved will help.

WHEN THEY SAY: *"Daddy won't play with me!"*

DON'T SAY: *"Please don't be selfish. We have to do what Daddy wants now."*

SAY: *"I'm sorry, honey. Daddy's sickness makes him tired. Let's let him rest a bit. You can check back in an hour and see if he feels more up to playing. How about you draw him a picture so you can show it to him when he wakes up?"*

BECAUSE: The child wants life to be back to normal. It's hard for her to accept that things have changed— especially that her dad has changed. It is scary to think he might be "different." Help her find new ways of "playing" with her dad.

WHEN THEY SAY: *"Why are you crying?"*

DON'T SAY: *"I have something in my eye."*

SAY: *"I am sad that Daddy is sick."*

BECAUSE: Children tune in to the emotional moods of the important adults in their lives. They watch, and read, the way parents non-verbally communicate. Even if adults think they are hiding it, it's likely the child knows what's happening, or at least that the mood in the house has shifted to one of worry and concern. If his mom hides or denies her worry, he might think there must be something really bad happening, and he might develop great fears but feel like he can't talk about them. It's best to communicate openly rather than denying your feelings. Just a short response is often enough. If adults go on and on about their worries in detail, this will be more than he can handle.

WHEN THEY SAY: *"Why does Daddy just lie there and not talk?"*

DON'T SAY: *"Daddy is going to take a long sleep soon."*

SAY: *"Daddy is going to die soon, and his body will be taken away. I think you should say goodbye to Daddy today."*

BECAUSE: If the child is told Daddy is going to sleep, she will feel confused and know that it's false when Daddy doesn't wake up. She might express anger at being tricked (and robbed of the chance to say goodbye even though she can't articulate it). She needs to be told the truth before death comes so that in her own way, she can say goodbye and part with her father.

SCHOOL-AGERS—AGES 6 TO 11

Talking to school-aged children about a terminal or life-threatening illness

---

WHEN THEY SAY: *"Is he going to die?"*

DON'T SAY: *"No, he's going to get better. I just know it."*

SAY: *"We don't know the answer to that yet. He has terminal cancer. Terminal means that the doctors don't have a cure for it. But sometimes people who have terminal diseases live longer than expected— sometimes months and maybe even years. The doctors are doing everything they can to make that happen for Dad. I will tell you when I know more about his situation."*

BECAUSE: It is a challenge to know what's best to tell a child about terminal illness. On the one hand, they should know there's a fair chance their father will die. On the other, if they are given a number, like three months, and it really is longer in the end, have you caused unneeded worry or distracted the child from enjoying the time he has with his father—or final adventures the family might experience? Here is where you, as the companion, need to gauge the child's developmental stage and emotional and cognitive development—along with her personal temperament—and decide just how much information this unique child can handle.

WHEN THEY SAY: *"I don't want to go to the hospital! The hospital stinks!"*

DON'T SAY: *"You have no choice. We are all going to support him and be by his side."*

SAY: *"How about you think it over for the next half hour*

and give me your answer then? If you still don't want to go, I'll call Ethan's mom and see if you can go to their house for a while. You can always go to the hospital next time."

BECAUSE: The child may feel overwhelmed by the hospital. It might remind him that Dad is sick and dying—a reality he isn't ready to face or doesn't want to face today. Respect his hesitancy and the fact that it feels too big for him to handle right now. The child can't accept his new reality until he is ready. He may be temporarily in denial, and that's OK. Remember, there is no "right" way to grieve, and grieving is messy. It's even messier when we assign guilt to it.

WHEN THEY SAY: *"What's going to happen?"*

DON'T SAY: *"I don't know how we are going to manage it all!"*

SAY: *"We will do our best to keep life as normal as possible. You will go to school as usual. You'll go to gymnastics practice and do swim team. We will have to juggle our schedules with his treatment schedule, but we will do our best to make it work. Lots of people have offered to help."*

BECAUSE: Stability is important right now for the child. She needs to know her entire life hasn't blown up due to the family member's illness. Having her usual routine will provide comfort. However, she should also understand how treatment will affect her life—how routines will change and who will be in charge of what. Also, tell her how treatment will affect the person who is ill—how he will be tired, sick, lose his hair after chemo, etc.

WHEN THEY SAY: *"I'm scared."*

DON'T SAY: *"Don't be scared. It's gonna be OK."*

SAY: *"Sometimes I get scared too. Can we take a walk around the block and talk about it?"*
OR:
"It's really normal for kids to feel scared when someone they love is dying. Sometimes it helps to talk with other kids in the same situation. I heard from hospice about a grief group for kids. Would you like to go once and see what it is like?"

BECAUSE: When a family member is ill, things change quickly in the household. Adjusting to the new roles—for example, mom having to work more, kids having to join a carpool, caretakers being in the house, etc. can leave kids feeling confused and disconnected. The life they once knew is changing, and that's scary. Death is also an unknown and often carries frightening connotations for kids, as it's not usually presented as just a normal part of life, but something to be avoided at all costs. Research shows that instilling a sense that death and dying are normal parts of life is helpful, and healthy, for kids.

TEENAGERS—AGES 12 TO 19
Talking to teenagers about a terminal or life-threatening illness

WHEN THEY SAY: *"I wish Dad would die. It's so hard to see him in pain!"*

DON'T SAY: *"How dare you say that! He's your father!"*

SAY: *"I agree; it's really hard to watch him suffer. I know you want him around, but not like this. How about the next time he feels better we take him out to his favorite spot down by the lake? You know, where we used to picnic when you were little?"*

BECAUSE: When someone we love is diagnosed with a terminal illness, we begin our grieving process before the death. It's called anticipatory grief. In some ways, the teen might be ready for his father to die. He may have accepted the reality of the death, and now is concerned about prolonging it, especially when it's painful. When death comes, he might even feel relief. This is normal and in no way equals a lack of love for the person who died. On the other hand, despite his anticipatory grief, he will likely experience a renewed sense of shock and numbness when Dad dies. This is normal. We're never truly "ready" for death. For now, focus on quality of life as best you can. Arrange events and conversations that reinforce a sense of life coming full circle—visiting favorite spots, having talks about the future with Dad weighing in, seeing important friends and family, and celebrating birthdays and holidays.

WHEN THEY SAY: *"This isn't fair! Why does this have to happen to us?!"*

DON'T SAY: *"You are the oldest. I need you to be strong right now."*

SAY: *"I hear your frustration. It is really hard to watch someone you love die and feel so helpless about it.*

Other families have had to go through this too.
Come here and let me hold you."

BECAUSE: More than anger, the teen is feeling overwhelmed by the burden and agonizing pain of watching someone she loves die. She may also be feeling afraid about the future, which is on hold while her family member is sick, and what it will mean for her to live without the person. Accept her questions and fears. When you do, you send the message that you accept her. This is critical because grieving young people can be extremely sensitive to even the slightest hint of rejection. Under her fear and anger is a need for warmth, acceptance, comfort, and understanding.

WHEN THEY SAY: *"I just gotta get out of here. Don't expect me home tonight. I'm going to Zach's house."*

DON'T SAY: *"You need to stick around. We have to be here for each other."*

SAY: *"It sounds like you need a break. I can respect that, but please make good choices. You seem really upset right now, and I don't want you to react and do something unsafe. Check in with me later, OK?"*

BECAUSE: Mourning the pending death of a family member is extra complicated for teens. They developmentally need to separate from their families, yet they feel conflicted when someone in the family is dying. These two disagreeing needs lay the groundwork for feelings of guilt and a desire to "escape," possibly by taking unneeded risks. This is especially true if the relationship between the dying person and teen is strained, or the teen has been rebellious in the past. Stay involved in the teen's life. Initiate open, honest, healthy talks to clear the air between the dying person and the teen.

WHEN THEY SAY: *"I know it's stupid, but I'm mad at him for dying!"*

DON'T SAY: *"You are right. That is kind of stupid. You know he can't help it."*

SAY: *"Actually, I get it. I have even felt angry at times. How can he leave us when we still need him so much and there is so much still ahead of us? It doesn't matter if it's rational to feel this way. It's real!"*

BECAUSE: Teens, and anyone grieving, need to know that there are no "wrong" or "right" feelings. Commiserating with her will make her feel less alone and sends a powerful message of acceptance.

WHEN THEY SAY: *"I don't know how I will go on without him."*

DON'T SAY: *"You are going to have to find some inner strength."*

SAY: *"I believe in you, and I know you will find a way. I know it seems hard to imagine life without him, but we will mourn and remember together, and it will get easier as years pass. You will always have me. I plan to be here a long, long time."*

BECAUSE: Teens can have a strong need to push away painful realities. He needs reassurance right now that he will be able to survive this death. Teenagers look to the future more than younger children do, and they think about important milestones, like graduating from high school, attending college, getting married, and having children. The idea that the person won't be there to witness these big events is disappointing and worrisome for teens. When these events do arrive, his grief may return afresh.

"There is no foot too small that it cannot
leave an imprint on the world."

— AUTHOR UNKNOWN

CHAPTER ELEVEN

When the child is dying

Helping a child face death may be the hardest thing you will ever
have to do. Children are not supposed to die; everyone carries
an intrinsic denial that such an unbelievable thing can happen.
You may grapple with the unfairness of it and feel remorse that
the potential of the child's life will be cut short. Even if you can
only accept the death in your head now, that's OK. It may not be
until after the death that you integrate it into your heart. While
you sit by the child's side, remember that she has the capacity to
understand more than you might think. Children of almost any
age can cope with what they know. They can't cope with what
they don't know. She deserves your respect and compassion—and
your honesty. When death nears, let her know that she will
likely die, in language she can understand. No doubt this will be
difficult, but hiding her death robs her of the chance to reconcile it
within herself as best she can, and gives her the privilege of saying
goodbye. Of course, you will address the matter in words she can
understand and in amounts she can handle at one time. Finally,
talking with dying children will require you to get clear on your
own beliefs about death, dying, and the afterlife. It will encourage
you to tap into your spirituality and call on your religious beliefs
to answer questions with hope and honesty.

PRESCHOOLERS—AGES 3 TO 5

Talking to preschoolers who are dying

WHEN THEY SAY: *"What's wrong with me?"*

DON'T SAY: *"Oh, just a little sickness. You will be better in no time."*

SAY: *"You have a disease that is hurting your body. You didn't do anything wrong to get it. Sometimes, people's bodies just stop working right."*
OR/AND:
"We, and the doctors, are doing everything we can to make you well, but you are very sick. We want you to live more than anything in the whole world, but we are not 100 percent sure that you will."

BECAUSE: According to respected pediatricians, children as young as three can be aware of a terminal prognosis even if an adult doesn't tell them about it. If you avoid telling a child, he may be left feeling abandoned or sense your worry and feel a need to protect you and make you feel better, rather than the other way around. Even though it is exceptionally hard, do your best to be honest. A study by a group of pediatricians, Kreicbergs et al., found that none of the surveyed parents regretted talking to their dying child about death, but a third of those who didn't talk had regrets and wished they would have done so. Most sensed that their child was aware of his imminent death.

WHEN THEY SAY: *"What is dying?" Or, "What is dead?"*

DON'T SAY: *"Oh, let's not talk about that. Look, I got you a new Barbie doll!"*

SAY: *"Every living thing dies. Bugs die when you squish them. Squirrels die when they get hit by cars. Even people die. Remember when Grammie Anderson* *died? Dying means that you are no longer alive to talk, jump around, and play. Your body just simply stops working."*

BECAUSE: If the child is asking about dying, she has awareness that she may be dying and she wants to understand what is happening to her. If you ignore her question or distract her, she will feel your dishonesty, which will make her feel alone and only prove to heighten any fears or anxiety that she is carrying. Since children live in the world of feelings, when you withhold your feelings or the truth, they know it and may feel separated from you.

WHEN THEY SAY: *"Mommy, it hurts!"*

DON'T SAY: *"I am sorry. I don't know what to do. Can you be brave?"*

SAY: *"I will talk with the doctor to see if he can give you some special medicine to make the pain go away. Come here and let me hold you. Can I rub your legs and arms? That might make you feel better."*

BECAUSE: With some childhood diseases and required treatments, the child might be in physical pain. It is very hard for parents to watch their child suffer. Do what you can to promote pain relief but then simply offer comfort.

WHEN THEY SAY: *"I just want to go home! Take me home!"*

DON'T SAY: *"You need to calm down! The doctors say we can't leave."*

SAY: *"Are you scared to be in the hospital, honey? I know it is big and you would rather be home, but did you know all the people here care about you and are working to make you better? Plus, Mommy and Daddy are going to take turns and stay with you all the time. Do you see that chair over there? It unfolds into a bed for us to sleep on."*

BECAUSE: Hospitals are big and white and scary to young children. Reassure him that you will stay with him. Introduce him to the hospital staff, if they don't do so on their own. Ask the nurses if they have children, and ask the children's names so the child feels more trust toward his caregivers.

WHEN THEY SAY: *"Where will I go after I die?"*

DON'T SAY: *"I don't know, sweetie."*
OR:
"I wish we could be there with you, but we can't."

SAY: *"I believe that when we die we see a light and there is a huge bubble of love and happiness and warm air that surrounds us. I think this love is God. I also believe that when we die we are reunited with the spirits of the people we love and know who died before us. That means that you will be with Grandpa Steve again. I bet he will love taking care of you."*

BECAUSE: Naturally the child is feeling a fear of both separation from you and a fear of the unknown. The fact that we die alone might be the most frightening fact of all about death. Since no one has proof of exactly what happens after we die, tap into your own beliefs, religious or otherwise, and share them with her. Share the positive outcomes to death as you see them. Even if you don't believe in an afterlife, you can talk about how after death there is no pain. You can admit you are unsure of what happens, if you are, and instead share a few common beliefs about what happens after death. For very young children, especially, the goal is to offer reassurance. And don't forget to ask the child what *she* believes. She may have more insight than you can imagine.

SCHOOL-AGERS—AGES 6 TO 11

Talking to school-aged children who are dying

WHEN THEY SAY: *"Am I going to die?"*

DON'T SAY: *"We don't want to think about that."*

SAY: *"It sounds like you want to talk about what might happen if you don't get better. Tell me more about what is on your mind."*

BECAUSE: Asking an open-ended question gives the child a chance to tell you what he is thinking and to also decide if he really wants, or is ready for, an answer to the question at this time.

WHEN THEY SAY: *"Can I talk to (see you, be with) you after I die?"*

DON'T SAY: *"I know this is hard to hear, but no. I wish it wasn't true, but it is."*

SAY: *"We can't be together like we are now, but do you know how we talked about how there are three parts to us—our bodies, our minds, and our souls (or spirits)? Our bodies can't be together, or our minds, but I believe that our souls/spirits will always stay connected by an invisible string of love."*

BECAUSE: Separation is unbearable for the child as well as for those who are left behind. Releasing a child into the unknown is counter to every bone in your parenting body. While physically you will be separated, you may believe that spiritually you will still be connected. If this is true, answer with honesty and hope.

WHEN THEY SAY: *"What is heaven like?" Or, "Where do I go after I die?"*

DON'T SAY: *"No one knows for sure. It is a mystery."*

SAY: *"Here is what I believe...."*

BECAUSE: The child wants real answers to an impossible question—what happens after we die. Be honest about your beliefs about what happens after we die. Keep your explanation as positive as possible. If you need help, look for resources to guide this discussion—a hospice nurse or a children's book such as *The Next Place*, by Warren Hanson, or *Tell Me About Heaven*, by Randy Alcorn and Ron Dicianni, are some options.

WHEN THEY SAY: *"Will you forget me after I die?"*

DON'T SAY: *"We will find a way to go on."*

SAY: *"We will all be very sad, but we will never forget you. We will keep you alive in our hearts and our memories forever."*

AND:
"Let's make a special memory book of your life. You can tell us what you think we should put in there to remember you, OK?"

AND:
"What do you want to do with your special belongings?"

AND:
"Who do you want to say goodbye to or talk to before the time comes?"

BECAUSE: Just as adults have a desire to "wrap things up" before they die, so do children. Imagine all the things you settle before moving or going on an extended trip. You tend to call the people closest to you to say goodbye or have coffee with before you

leave. You get your house in order and settle any
outstanding projects or obligations. It is somewhat
similar when you die. Help the child do these
final tasks, but especially help her make the final
connections or say her final goodbyes to people she
cares about. Let her participate in making memory
boxes, scrapbooks of favorite times, and writing
letters to her loved ones. Doing so helps her feel
more "ready" to die and more at peace.

WHEN THEY SAY: *"I think I am ready to die."*

DON'T SAY: *"Don't give up! Focus on living!"*

SAY: *"I hear you, and as impossible as it seems, I am
starting to think that too. I know you have been in
great pain. I want you to know that when you are
ready to die, I'll let you. I will be OK. Everyone in
our family will be OK. When the time comes, I will
be right here by your side, holding your hand."*
OR/AND:
*"Of course I will miss you while I am still here on
Earth, but I know I will see you again in heaven."*

BECAUSE: Dying children can feel a heightened sense of
responsibility to live for their parents. They are
programmed to not disappoint them and "do what
they are told." If a child is near the end of his life
and he voices a desire to die, honor it. Everything
inside of you might be shouting, "NO!", but try
to tap into that voice of wisdom that knows the
truth—that it is time for your child to die—and
respond from that place. Giving your dying child
permission to leave you will be unbearably and
unthinkably difficult, but it is a gift of love to do so.

TEENAGERS—AGES 12 TO 19
Talking to teenagers who are dying

WHEN THEY SAY: *"What's wrong with me? Why can't I get better?"*

DON'T SAY: *"Don't worry. You are going to get better. I just know it."*

SAY: *"We have tried every possible treatment to help you get well. Right now, the doctors don't know of anything else we can do. How about we do some of our own research on your illness? It will help us understand it better, maybe learn about other kids your age with the same illness, and see if we can find any more options. Do you want me to bring in the laptop?"*

BECAUSE: Inviting her to participate in learning about her illness or disease will at least help her understand it—and when we understand things, we are not quite so afraid of them. Trying to find solutions will help fulfill her need to solve the problem, even if the answer is that there is nothing to do. Going through the process will prepare her a bit more for accepting that she is dying.

WHEN THEY SAY: *"I'll do anything to live!"*

DON'T SAY: *"We decided that another round of chemotherapy will make you too weak and possibly hurt more than it will help, so you can't do it."*
OR:
"Don't worry, we are not going to let you die!"

SAY: *"The doctors have discussed the possible risks and benefits of more chemotherapy. This is what they are.... Here is what we think.... What do you think?"*

BECAUSE: A teen has a right to make decisions about his own care, especially when those decisions can have life-or-death consequences. Including him in these tough, often complicated decisions—which have no clear wrong or right answers—shows respect and puts him in the driver's seat of his own life. He doesn't have much control over anything right now, and he deserves this chance to feel empowered. He is feeling desperate to live, which is completely normal. Terminally ill people may know they are dying, but it is human nature to want to live. Of course, listen to his regret, disappointment, and desperate desire, and share your own, but start thinking on more spiritual terms of encouraging his acceptance, and being open to your own, if death is likely.

WHEN THEY SAY: *"I can't believe this is happening to me. I am so scared!"*

DON'T SAY: *"It's just not right! You shouldn't have to die!"*

SAY: *"I understand you are scared. I am scared too. But I will be right here by your side the whole time. We will go through this together."*

BECAUSE: As hard as it may seem, a part of your job as a companion is to help the child accept, and prepare for, death. You are not going to want to "give up," but at some point you may have to set aside your strong feelings of protest over her death while in her presence. Do your best to tap into her needs and be fully present to her as she dies. When not by her side, seek out your own companion—someone who is not afraid to hear your raw pain and will accept you and support you no matter what you say, feel, or do.

WHEN THEY SAY: *"Why me? Why do I have to die?!"*

DON'T SAY: *"Let's not think about it. Let's do something fun instead, like watching that new comedy I heard about."*

SAY: *"I don't know. I don't know why you got leukemia. It is nothing you did, and of course it doesn't feel fair. I wish it wasn't happening, but it is and we can't change that. I love you so much."*

BECAUSE: Before any acceptance can come, the teen will have to grapple with "Why" and "If only," and "I don't want to die!" Avoiding these hard, hard discussions will not make her pain go away. Accompany her and her suffering. Help her move beyond the confusion, anger, fear, and sadness she is bound to feel toward acceptance, so she can die with some peace in her heart.

"When words are inadequate, have a ceremony."

— DR. ALAN WOLFELT

CHAPTER TWELVE

Attending a funeral or ceremony

Much of this book has encouraged you, the child's companion, to be honest with him as he grapples to understand death and share his feelings of grief. I've also promoted that you include him in discussions and activities that allow him to access his feelings and find a variety of ways, including asking questions, to express them. With that said, funerals and ceremonies are fertile ground for encouraging the release of grief—mourning—and inviting open discussions about death. To help with healing, I encourage you to not only allow him to attend, but participate in his loved one's funeral or ceremony if he wants. In doing so, you help him fulfill his innate desire to say goodbye and witness his raw and heartfelt love and missing of the person to others. The funeral is the first of many goodbyes.

Yes, meaningful funerals that invite open mourning by asking people to express their emotions are painful. Please remember that pain is not the enemy. While it never feels good to hurt, entering pain and facing it eventually brings some relief and lets us integrate the death into our lives. Children, then, are given the chance, with the help of loving adults, to rearrange the pieces of their lives and put them together in a way that lets them live a meaningful life without the person who died. If denied this chance, the child may feel lost and insecure in his world. You don't have to have just one funeral. It's healing to have ceremonies or simple rituals to honor your loved one for as long as you need to or want to. Such rituals can be as simple as toasting the person who died at Christmas time or sitting in the garden listening to the wind chimes you bought in her memory.

PRESCHOOLERS—AGES 3 TO 5
Talking to preschoolers about funerals

WHEN THEY SAY: *"What is a funeral?"*

DON'T SAY: *"You are too young to go, so don't worry about it. We will have Jamie come babysit you."*

SAY: *"A funeral is when friends and family get together and remember the person who died."*
OR/AND:
"Here is what happens at a funeral. We go to a church (etc.) and sit quietly with other people who knew and cared about Uncle Ned. People will take turns talking about Uncle Ned, singing, and reading poems or telling stories about him. Some people will be crying. At times, people may laugh. We have to stay seated and put on good listening ears. There is also a time when we can say goodbye to Uncle Ned's body in the casket. Does that sound like something you would like to be part of?"

BECAUSE: Attending a funeral is a new and strange experience for young children. The event tends to go better for the child when she knows what to expect and what behavior is expected of her.

WHEN THEY SAY: *"Can Grandma hear me in her casket?"*

DON'T SAY: *"You can talk to Grandma and tell her how much you will miss her."*

SAY: *"No. Grandma can't hear you or see you or feel your touch. She is dead. When bodies die, they don't work anymore. She can't feel anything. We can see her to say goodbye to her body, but you should know she won't look the same as she did when she was alive."*
OR/AND:
"If you think you want to see Grandma's body, you can come to the visitation today with everyone else, or if you want I can take just you this morning so you can say goodbye by yourself."

BECAUSE: Sometimes preschoolers imagine that Grandma is alive in a box with the lid closed. Remind him that it is just Grandma's body that is here now, and it doesn't work, or look, how it did when it was alive. Give him the option to view the body, or not, and touch the body, or not.

WHEN THEY SAY: *"What if Grandma wakes up underground and can't breathe?"*

DON'T SAY: *"Grandma is not really there. She is in heaven."*

SAY: *"Grandma's body stopped working, and it can't start working again. Her body doesn't feel anything in its casket."*
YOU CAN ADD:
"It is only her body that is in the casket. Her spirit— the part that made her laugh, smile, love, and enjoy you, is in heaven."

BECAUSE: Since preschoolers may not understand that death is final, you need to make it clear that when someone dies, she can't come back to life. You can use a version of this explanation when a young child asks "What is death?" If you hold a religious belief that souls are released from the body and ascend to heaven, you can share this with the child, but know she might get confused by this abstract idea. She is simply too young to understand. That's OK. She will gain more understanding as she grows. Just be willing to answer her ongoing questions and observe her ongoing death play as she continues to explore this idea.

WHEN THEY SAY: *"How can I say goodbye to Grandpa if he's dead?*

DON'T SAY: *"Grandpa wants to hear you say goodbye to him. He is up in heaven listening."*

SAY: *"It sounds funny, but we say goodbye to the dead body to make us feel better, not so that Grandpa can hear us. It is our chance to say out loud why we love Grandpa and why we will miss him. But you don't have to do it if you don't want to. And if you choose to touch Grandpa or give him a kiss, you should know his body is really cold and he can't respond like he did when he was alive."*

BECAUSE: Even if the preschooler might not completely understand death, it is OK to let him experience it. He will store it away and over time draw on it as a reference on death. He doesn't need to totally understand why it is healing to say goodbye to Grandpa, or shed tears about Grandpa dying. The healing will happen regardless. Preparing him so that it is an acceptable and "open" experience instead of a frightening and "secret" one is wise.

SCHOOL-AGERS—AGES 6 TO 11

Talking to school-aged children about funerals

WHEN THEY SAY: *"What is cremation?"*

DON'T SAY: *"After Aunt Sue dies, we will burn her body."*

SAY: *"The body is put in a room with lots of heat until it turns to ashes."*

AND:

"What's left of the body looks like kind of like kitty litter except it's white or gray like bone. The crematory, where they cremate the body, gives the family the ashes, and we can sprinkle them on the ground in places that were special to Aunt Sue, like up at her cabin. They can help the wildflowers grow."

BECAUSE: Cremation is a strange concept. If needed, read about it yourself first. Share that it is an ancient tradition that has been used for thousands of years. Make sure he understands that the person is dead and that she doesn't feel pain or anything at all during cremation.

WHEN THEY SAY: *"I can't believe they burn her! That is terrible!"*

DON'T SAY: *"You don't understand. Please calm down."*

SAY: *"I know it sounds weird, and even mean, but it's not. The people doing the cremation take it very seriously and handle the body with a lot of respect. Just like you, they know that Aunt Sue was special and that she deserves to leave this world with dignity."*

BECAUSE: The idea of cremation can be a scary one for children. Let him know he can ask anything he wants to about the cremation process. Assure him that it was what the person he loved wanted, that she knew it wouldn't hurt, and that she liked the idea of her ashes being shared with the people she loved.

WHEN THEY SAY: *"I want to see his body."*

DON'T SAY: *"No. The viewing is just for adults."*

SAY: *"That is your choice. I want you there too. It is a good way for everyone who loved Ellie to say goodbye to her. Even though her spirit has left, her body is still here. The funeral home dressed her in her favorite dress, but you should know her face will look different and may surprise you."*

BECAUSE: Some parents fear that if a child sees the dead body, it will become the last "memory picture" of the person who died. Yes, maybe that image will come up when the child thinks of the person, but others of good times shared will too. It is in seeing someone dead that we truly begin to acknowledge the death and appropriately shift the relationship to one of memory. Seeing the dead body of someone we have loved is often the beginning of a more essential, active grief process.

WHEN THEY SAY: *"I don't want to go to the funeral!"*

DON'T SAY: *"You have to."*

SAY: *"OK. But can I tell you about what happens at funerals and why we have them first? Then after you think about it, you can give me your final answer."*

BECAUSE: The idea of funerals may be strange to some children. He might have a preconceived, and scary, notion of funerals. Help him understand what funerals are all about. Let him know it is a time to say goodbye with others who want to say goodbye too. Explain it is a time to honor the person who died. Let him know that sometimes when we are sad, it helps to be around others who are sad, and that together we can comfort each other and help each other feel a little better or a little less alone. If you want, explain your religious traditions around funerals in easy-to-understand terms. If he still doesn't want to go, don't force it. Offer another option for him to say goodbye.

TEENAGERS—AGES 12 TO 19
Talking to teenagers about funerals

WHEN THEY SAY: *"I'm not ready to say goodbye. He can't be gone.
I have too much I still need to say."*

DON'T SAY: *"It's OK. You don't have to go to the funeral."*

SAY: *"Can you tell me more about that?"*
AND:
*"Please know that the funeral is just the first
of many goodbyes."*

BECAUSE: There may be feelings of guilt or regret that are
complicating the teen's ability to face the death.
Maybe he is remembering a fight he had with
the person who died shortly before the death,
or maybe he is haunted by an unresolved issue
between them. He may wish for a chance to do
things differently, take back words, or get along
better. Reassure him that while he can't go back
and change things, he and the person who died
had a complex yet loving relationship and that
disagreements are normal when we are entwined
with another. Explain that squabbles are like
rolling waves on the surface and that the vast
majority of the connection between them was
calm and deep. Give examples of how the core
of their relationship was built on love, and help
him trust that the person who died would be as
understanding in death as he was in life.

WHEN THEY SAY: *"So we have the funeral, and that's it?
There is nothing else?"*

DON'T SAY: *"The funeral gives us closure. We can put his death
behind us and move on after that."*

SAY: *"It sounds like you'd like to honor Sam in some way that's meaningful. Do you want to participate in the funeral? You could read a poem, talk about what Sam meant to you, write a letter and put it in his casket, bring pictures of you two to put in the lobby, or make a goodbye card to display. Or if you'd rather do something private like make a scrapbook of Sam's life or have a private family ceremony afterwards, we can do that too. Does any of that appeal to you?"*

BECAUSE: The teen wants to let the world know that the person who died mattered to her. Help her find her own unique way to say goodbye at, or after, the funeral. Let her know that whatever she thinks of is fine and that you will try your best to make it happen—even if it is a big undertaking, like organizing an event in the person's name. Let the teen lead.

WHEN THEY SAY: *"I want to participate, but it is too hard. I am too sad."*

DON'T SAY: *"How about I put you down for just a short poem."*

SAY: *"I hear you. Does it just feel too big right now and you are feeling too emotional? How about we have a candle ceremony, just our family? If we want to talk we can, or we can just sit quietly and remember her silently. How does that sound?"*

BECAUSE: I like the saying, "When words are inadequate, have a ceremony." Death can leave us speechless. The funeral is an important ritual, but there are no rules about it being the only one. It's OK, and even wise, to have as many rituals, big or small, planned or spontaneous, as the family wants to honor or say goodbye to the person who died. Rituals are a chance to provide physical closeness and comfort, which is reassuring to children during times of distress. What you say may not be as important as the touch or hugs you give.

WHEN THEY SAY: *"I can't face people at the funeral."*

DON'T SAY: *"Well you need to go. How would it look if his own daughter isn't there?"*

SAY: *"Why? Is there something you think you should feel ashamed about?"*
AND:
"People do not blame you. His death was not your fault. I think if you go, you'll see that people will just want to give you love and support."

BECAUSE: Developmentally, the teen is diving into abstract thought. She is forming philosophies and looking for meanings to make sense of life, the world, and the way things are. She spends hours and hours talking to friends and in class exploring justice, injustice, and forming ideas and observations. She's exploring religious and spiritual beliefs. With all these new thoughts and ideas, she may get moody or seemingly overly emotional. She may also travel down the road of a wild idea and get stuck in it. For example, she may think that because she chose to stay late at the party and drink and her dad had to come get her, that cosmically she is being punished for "being bad" and as a result of, say, "bad karma," her dad was killed in a car accident. Reassure her that she did not cause her father's death. If this isn't the case and she doesn't want to go to the funeral, keep exploring by asking, "Why?" Getting support from others, and seeing how much others loved her father, will help her heal.

WHEN THEY SAY: *"I don't want to be reminded of how sad it is to have Grandpa gone, so I don't want to go."*

DON'T SAY: *"It's not that kind of funeral. We are going to have a celebration of life and just focus on the positive things and try to have fun. It is really more of a party than a funeral."*

SAY: *"It's true that funerals can be sad. Yet feeling sad, and expressing it, helps us feel better. I know it sounds weird, but it's true. It won't just be sad. We will share stories about Grandpa, and people will say goodbye in their own ways, like by singing his favorite song or reading a poem or passage he was fond of. It's really just a way to honor Grandpa."*

BECAUSE: Even if it is painful, and not something people readily sign up to do, it's important to keep the service focused on remembering versus forgetting. If people just "party" without allowing opportunities to cry or feel sad, they miss the chance to fully mourn the person who died. But it is important to accept the child's way of mourning.

THE LANGUAGE OF FUNERALS

Ashes
(also called
cremated
remains)
What is left of a dead body after cremation. Looks like chunky sand or fishbowl rocks except it's white or gray. People commonly refer to these as "ashes" because of the Biblical passage that says "from ashes to ashes, dust to dust." However, the remains don't really look like ashes, so it may be less confusing to the child if you refer to them as "cremated remains."

Burial
Placing the body (which is inside a casket or urn, if the body was cremated) into the ground.

Casket
A special box for burying a dead body.

Cemetery
A place where many dead bodies and ashes are buried.

Columbarium
A little building at a cemetery where ashes are stored. Kind of like a grave that's above the ground.

Cremation
The dead body is put in a special metal container that gets very hot inside. The heat burns away all of the body parts except some small pieces of bone.

Dead
When a person's body stops working. It doesn't see, hear, feel, eat, breathe, etc. anymore.

Funeral
A time when friends and families get together to say goodbye and remember the person who died.

Funeral home
A place where bodies are kept until they are buried or cremated.

Grave
The hole in the ground where the body or ashes are buried at the cemetery.

Obituary
A short article in the paper that tells about the person who died.

Scattering
When the dead person's cremated remains are respectfully scattered onto the ground or water (or sometimes in the air) at a place that was special to him or her.

Urn
A special container that holds the cremated person's ashes.

Viewing
The time when people can see the body of the person who died and say goodbye.

"Children are the living messages we
send to a time we will not see."

— JOHN W. WHITEHEAD

A final word

I am certain that you will be faced with many more questions
besides those I have presented in this book as you companion a
child through the death of someone loved or through her own
death. I hope the suggested words I've provided here will give you
a starting point for conversations about death.

When it comes to companioning, keep it simple. Most impor-
tantly, show up. You will not have all the answers, and that's OK.
Respond from your heart, with honesty and care. Don't listen to
your head when it says you should be false or sugarcoat words to
"protect" the child. Even though the truth can be hard to say, say it.
The child depends on your honesty and authenticity to make her
world feel safe and right.

Children operate on a level of feelings and emotions first and
logic second. There is a direct line between your feelings and
her feelings. You send out signals about your emotions and your

wellbeing. When she senses insincerity or falseness, she, in turn, feels insecure. To best companion, start with authenticity: Be your true self, your highest self, your best self, and respond with love and respect to whatever questions she may have about death and dying.

You may wonder how long the child's grief will last. If ideal conditions exist (which they rarely do) and the child is actively mourning his grief with the support of caring adults and family members, active mourning can still take a number of years. And even that lucky child will encounter intermittent mourning as he develops and reintegrates his grief experience at different milestones throughout his life. Remember—grief waits on welcome, not on time! My best counsel is this: Keep in mind that grief does not have a definite end. Only as the child participates in authentic mourning will it erupt less frequently. Strive to be a long-term stabilizer in the child's life as he grows and develops. Walk beside him and allow him to teach you about his grief journey.

Thank you for having the courage to truly, openly, and honestly be there for the child in your life. Because of you and other caring adults, he can go on to not just survive his loss, but thrive in a life of meaning and promise.